BLUEPRINTS
Design & Technology
Copymasters
Key Stage 2

Kate Bennington

Stanley Thornes (Publishers) Ltd

Do you receive **BLUEPRINTS NEWS**?

Blueprints is an expanding series of practical teacher's ideas books and photocopiable resources for use in primary schools. Books are available for separate infant and junior age ranges for every core and foundation subject, as well as for an ever widening range of other primary teaching needs. These include **Blueprints Primary English** books and **Blueprints Resource Banks**. **Blueprints** are carefully structured around the demands of National Curriculum in England and Wales, but are used successfully by schools and teachers in Scotland, Northern Ireland and elsewhere.

Blueprints provide:
- *Total curriculum coverage*
- *Hundreds of practical ideas*
- *Books specifically for the age range you teach*
- *Flexible resources for the whole school or for individual teachers*
- *Excellent photocopiable sheets – ideal for assessment and children's work profiles*
- *Supreme value.*

Books may be bought by credit card over the telephone and information obtained on **(01242) 577944**. Alternatively, photocopy and return this **FREEPOST** form to receive **Blueprints News**, our regular update on all new and existing titles. You may also like to add the name of a friend who would be interested in being on the mailing list.

Please add my name to the **BLUEPRINTS NEWS** mailing list.

Mr/Mrs/Miss/Ms _____

Home address _____

_____ Postcode _____

School address _____

_____ Postcode _____

Please also send **BLUEPRINTS NEWS** to:

Mr/Mrs/Miss/Ms _____

Address _____

_____ Postcode _____

To: Marketing Services Dept., Stanley Thornes Ltd, FREEPOST (GR 782), Cheltenham, GL50 1BR

Text © Kate Bennington Original line illustrations by Mark Dunn
© Stanley Thornes (Publishers)

The author would like to acknowledge the help and support of the Rutherford Appleton Laboratories, Parsons Down Junior School, the Berkshire Design Technology team, her family and friends, and above all, her husband, Steve.

First published in 1996
First published in new binding in 1998 by:
Stanley Thornes (Publishers) Ltd
Ellenborough House
Wellington Street
CHELTENHAM GL50 1YW
England

98 99 00 01 02 / 10 9 8 7 6 5 4 3 2 1

A catalogue record for this book is available from the British Library.

ISBN 0–7487–3414–7

Typeset by Tech-Set, Gateshead, Tyne & Wear
Printed and bound in Great Britain by
Redwood Books, Trowbridge, Wiltshire

CONTENTS

Pop-up mechanisms

Make two of these simple mechanisms.

A

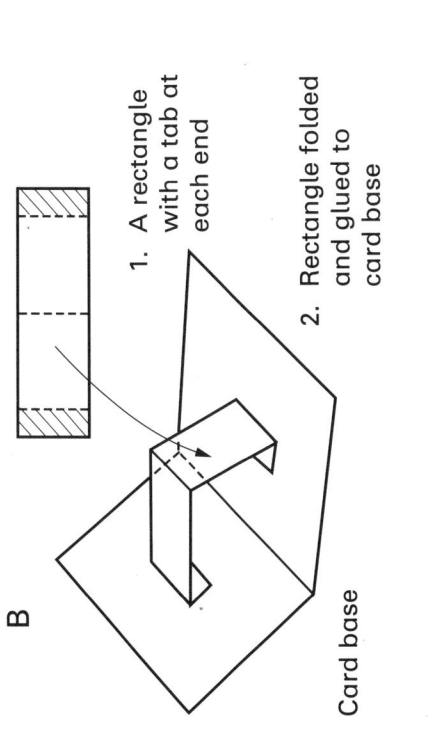

1. A card triangle with tabs
2. Folded and scored down the centre
3. Triangle folded and glued to card base

Card base

B

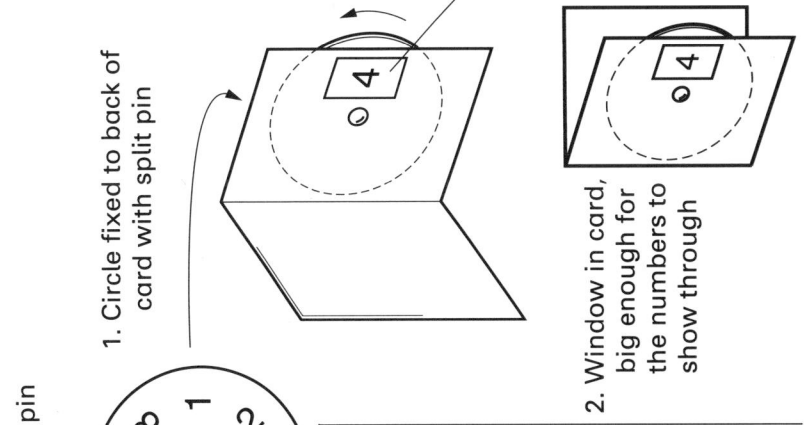

1. A rectangle with a tab at each end
2. Rectangle folded and glued to card base

Card base

C

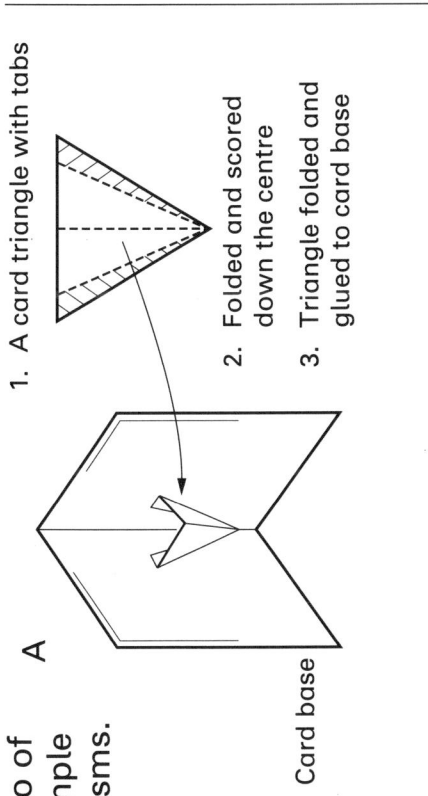

1. A strip of card with a tab at one end
2. Slots made in card base
3. Strip pushed through slots
4. Glue shape on to strip
5. Pull

Card base

D

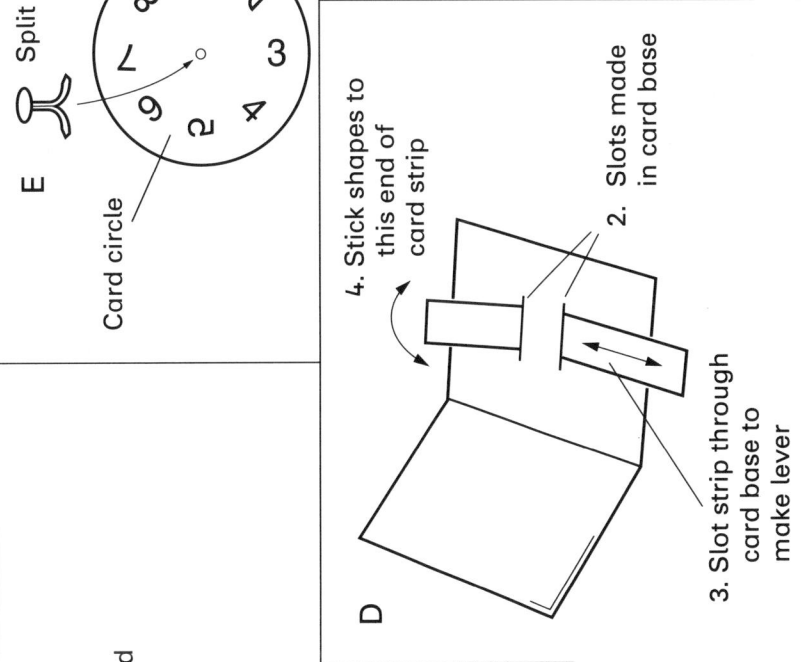

1. Fold and score a strip of card
2. Slots made in card base
3. Slot strip through card base to make lever
4. Stick shapes to this end of card strip

E

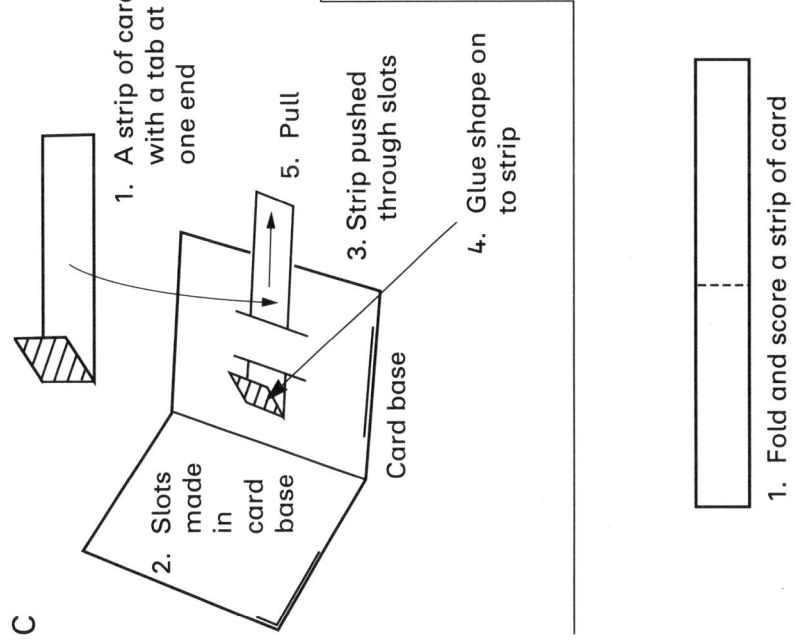

Split pin

Card circle

1. Circle fixed to back of card with split pin
2. Window in card, big enough for the numbers to show through

Making envelopes

Choose the design of envelope you like best (*Design* 1 or 2).
Follow the instructions to make an envelope for one of your cards.

Design 1

1. Put your card on to plain paper and draw around it.
2. Add on 1 cm all the way round.
3. Measure out and draw the centre lines (x and y) on your rectangle/square, as shown.
4. Add a triangle to each side of the shape, as shown.
5. Cut it out and fold where the dotted lines are marked below.
6. Glue all the flaps except A. (You need to be able to put your card inside the envelope.)

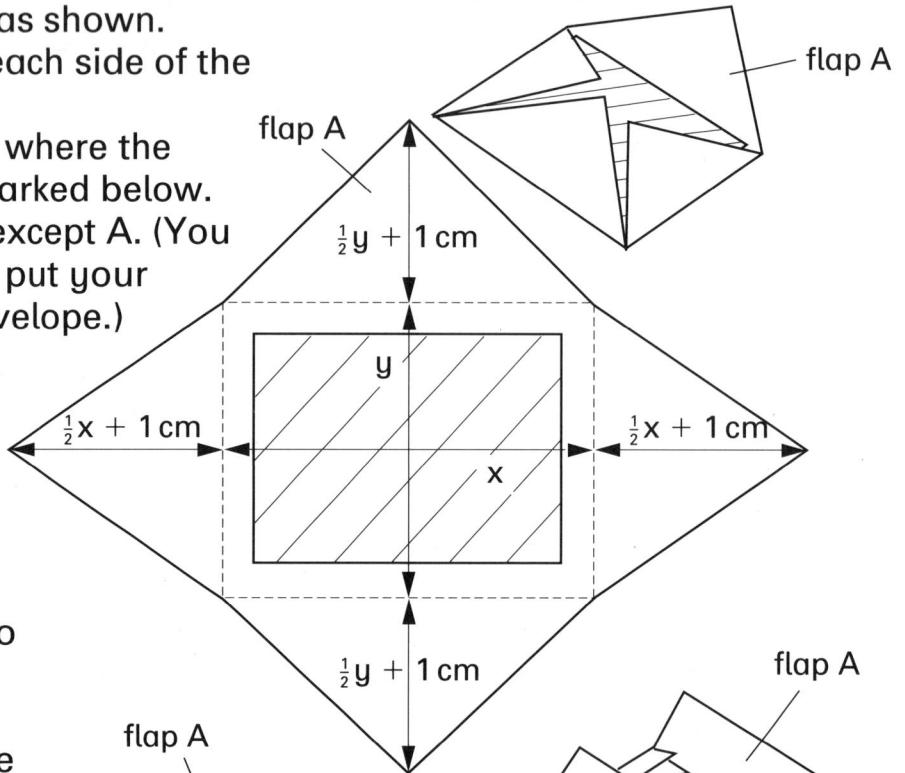

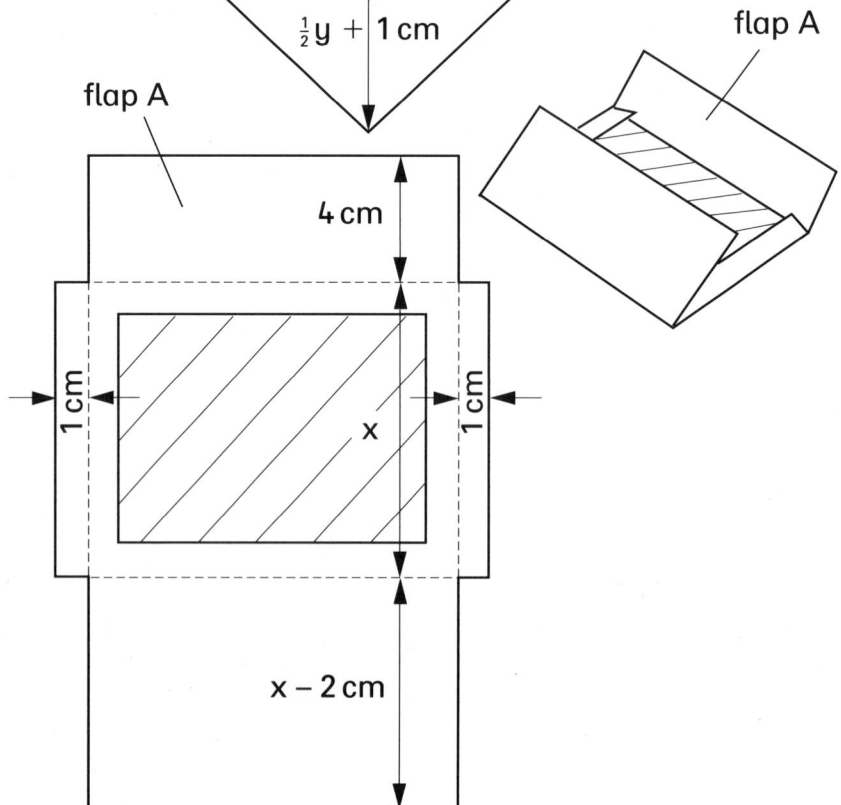

flap A

flap A

$\frac{1}{2}$y + 1 cm

y

$\frac{1}{2}$x + 1 cm

$\frac{1}{2}$x + 1 cm

x

$\frac{1}{2}$y + 1 cm

Design 2

1. Put your card on to plain paper and draw around it.
2. Add on 1 cm all the way round.
3. Measure the height of your rectangle/square (x).
4. Add on the extra rectangles, as shown.
5. Cut out the shape and fold where the dotted lines are marked below.
6. Glue all the flaps except A. (You need to be able to put your card inside the envelope.)

flap A

flap A

4 cm

1 cm

1 cm

x

x − 2 cm

Name _____

Ideas for pop-up cards

Rudolph

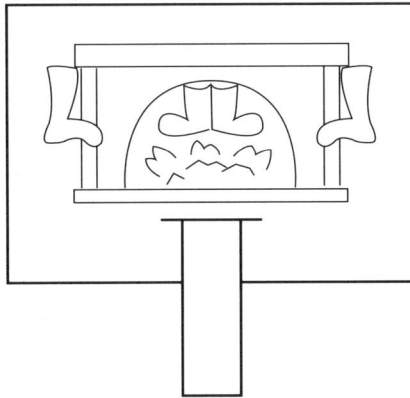

Father Christmas is coming...

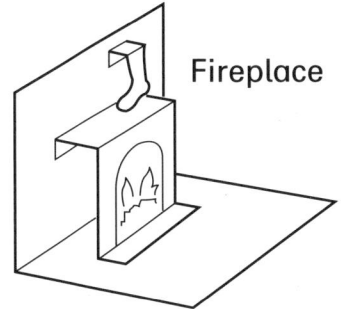

Fireplace

Pudding

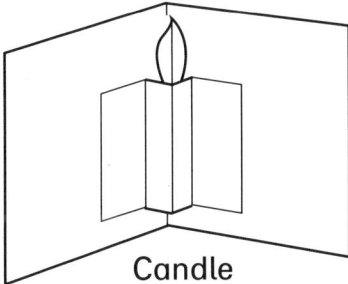

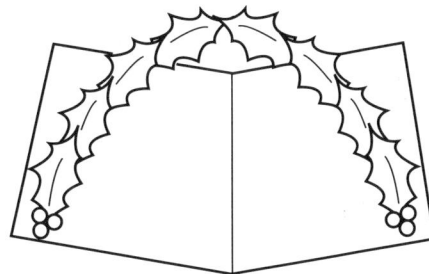

Holly bough

Candle

Angel

Menorah

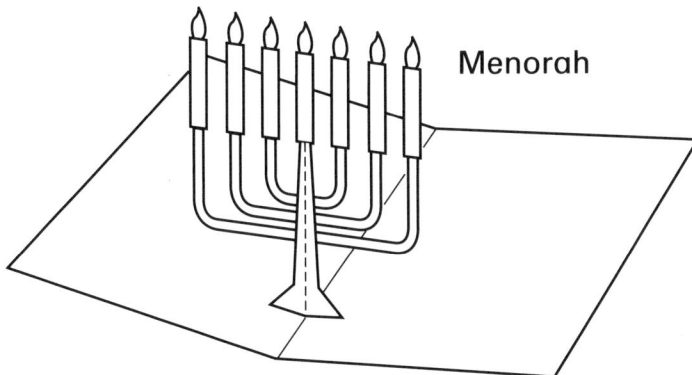

Follow the star

Copymaster 3

Name _____

Read the following passage about clocks.

Nowadays, clocks are everywhere – on buildings, in offices, on car dashboards and even on our wrists. But no-one is sure who invented the first clock. We know that ancient civilisations used a device called a water-clock to tell the time. (They worked out what time it was by measuring how much water had trickled from a container.) They also used sundials, but these were very difficult to read accurately.

As only a few people could use these instruments, towns and villages invented their own time signals. For example, bells would be rung to tell people when it was lunch-time or if a meeting was about to begin. Often the bells were not rung at exactly the right time but at least everyone got the message!

Mechanical clocks were not seen until the Middle Ages. We think that they were invented by monks. Before this invention, they had to ring the bells in the monastery chapel many times during the day and night to tell all the monks that it was time to pray. The clock was probably developed to make the ringing of the bells automatic. The first mechanical clock to be seen in Great Britain was built in Norwich Cathedral in 1325. A similar clock in St. Albans took about 30 years to build.

By 1550, spring-driven watches were small enough to carry, but they were still not very accurate. As industry increased and travel by coach became more common, it was necessary to keep to accurate timetables. This meant that there was a demand for accurate watches, and large clock- and watch-making shops grew up around Europe.

Now, answer these questions in sentences.

1. How did people from ancient civilisations tell the time?
2. How did communities know what the time was?
3. Who is believed to have invented mechanical clocks?
4. Why did the monks need to know the time so often?
5. Where was the first mechanical clock in Great Britain built?
6. How long did it take to build a mechanical clock in St Albans?
7. What was wrong with smaller watches in the 1550s?
8. Why did clocks have to become more accurate?

Name _____

Design and make a forex clock for a room in your house.

Here are some ideas for differently shaped clock faces.

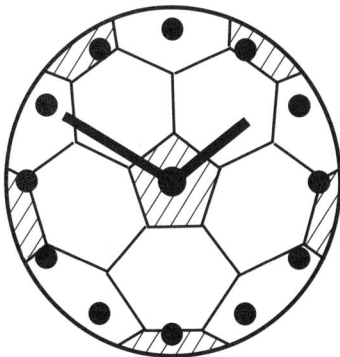

Before you start to design your clock, think about these things:

What is a clock? What is it used for?

Does a clock need to have a round face? What other shape could it be?

Do the hands need to be in the middle of the clock face?

What sort of numbers do you see on clock faces? Do all clock faces have numbers on them?

How are you going to decorate the clock face?

An exploded diagram of a clock mechanism

Hanger

Clock mechanism

Name _____

Houses and homes

Match the names to the correct pictures. The first one has been done for you.

Fort

Wigwam

House

Castle

Flats

Cottage

Caravan

Igloo

Draw pictures of who you think lives in these homes.

Barge

Name _____

Shells and frameworks

How do these objects keep their shape? Write whether each one has a shell or a frame.

Tent

Drinks can

jam

Jam jar

Pylon

WEETOS

Cereal packet

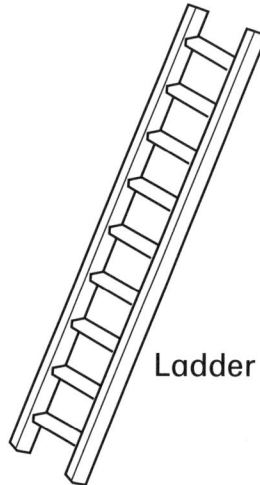

Ladder

Light bulb

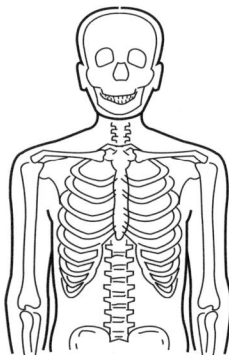

Skeleton

Bridge

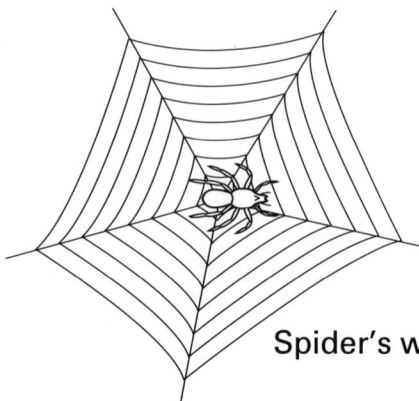

Spider's web

Snail

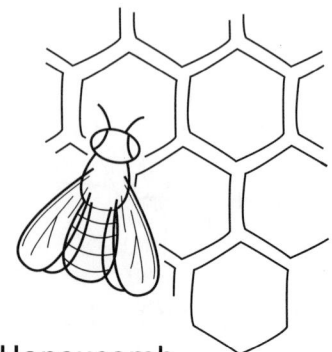

Honeycomb

Name _____

Design and make a paper tower that will hold a ping-pong ball as high off the floor as possible for 30 seconds. (You can use only one newspaper to build your tower.)

Read this sheet before you begin to design your tower. It should provide some helpful hints.

Designing
What shape will your tower be?
How will the Ping-Pong® ball be held in place?
(Remember to sketch your tower before you begin to build it.)

Making
What strong shapes could you include in the structure of your tower?
How are you going to join rolls of newspaper together?
How will you use the masking tape?

Evaluating
Is your tower as tall as you can make it?
Does it stand up on its own?
Could it have been made stronger?
Does the ball stay in place for long enough?
Could you make the ball more secure?
Can you improve the appearance of your tower?

Name _____

Up above ▷

Fill in the gaps in this passage using words from the box at the bottom of the page.

Roofs protect us from the weather. They keep us warm in ——— and cool in summer.

There are many different types of roofing ——— . Here are some of them.

Thatch

Thatch is made from ____ , and is pinned and sewn together. Thatchers sometimes cut it into patterns. In Britain, thatch is not used' very often because it is too _____ . Also, it needs to be _____ regularly, and wire netting must be put over the _____ to stop birds from _____in it.

Tiles

Roof tiles are made from ____ and come in different colours, shapes and sizes. The clay is different to the ____ made into bricks, but it is ——- in a similar way. Tiles are often used in ____ _____, and they are _____ to let the rain run off them.

Slate

Some roofs are made from a kind of _____ called slate, which is quarried out of the _____. Slate is made of many thin _____. It is cut into small sheets and _____ to the roof. The sheets are _____ so that the rain runs off them.

Roofing felt

Some roofs are flat and covered with sheets of _____felt. Sometimes, _____ collect on a flat roof, and so the _____ has to be checked and repaired regularly.

winter	ground	straw	nesting	repaired
thatch	clay	sort	Great Britain	puddles
channelled	stone	materials	layers	expensive
pinned	waterproof	baked	felt	overlapped

Copymaster 10

Name _____

Sailor Sam

Read this poem.

> Now Sam he was a sailor,
> He sailed the seven seas,
> He was at home on any ship,
> In gale or wind or breeze.
>
> Now as he went a-sailing,
> Across the ocean deep,
> A storm blew up. "Ahoy!" he cried,
> "How this old ship do creak!"
>
> The poor old ship, it tossed and rolled,
> Among the giant waves,
> Although the sailors clung on tight,
> Some went to watery graves.
>
> Now Sailor Sam was lucky,
> He drifted mile on mile,
> And then the ocean threw him up
> On a pleasant desert isle.
>
> He made himself a shelter,
> Of twigs and leaves and bark,
> And lit himself a cosy fire,
> For he did not like the dark!
>
> Although he's made a home there,
> He always is alone,
> And his message in a bottle says,
> "I'd like to get back home."
>
> *Sue Dillon*

Now, your task is to design a shelter for Sailor Sam.

Answer these questions. The answers should help you to design a good shelter.

1. How big does the shelter have to be?
2. How could you make it strong?
3. What shapes would you use to make it?
4. What materials might Sam find on the desert island to build his shelter?
5. What materials could *you* use to build a shelter?
6. How would Sam hold his shelter together?
7. What could *you* use to do the same thing?
8. How will Sam get in and out of his shelter?
9. How could it be made warm on the inside?
10. What happens if it rains? How could you make the shelter showerproof?

Name _____

Map of Sam's island

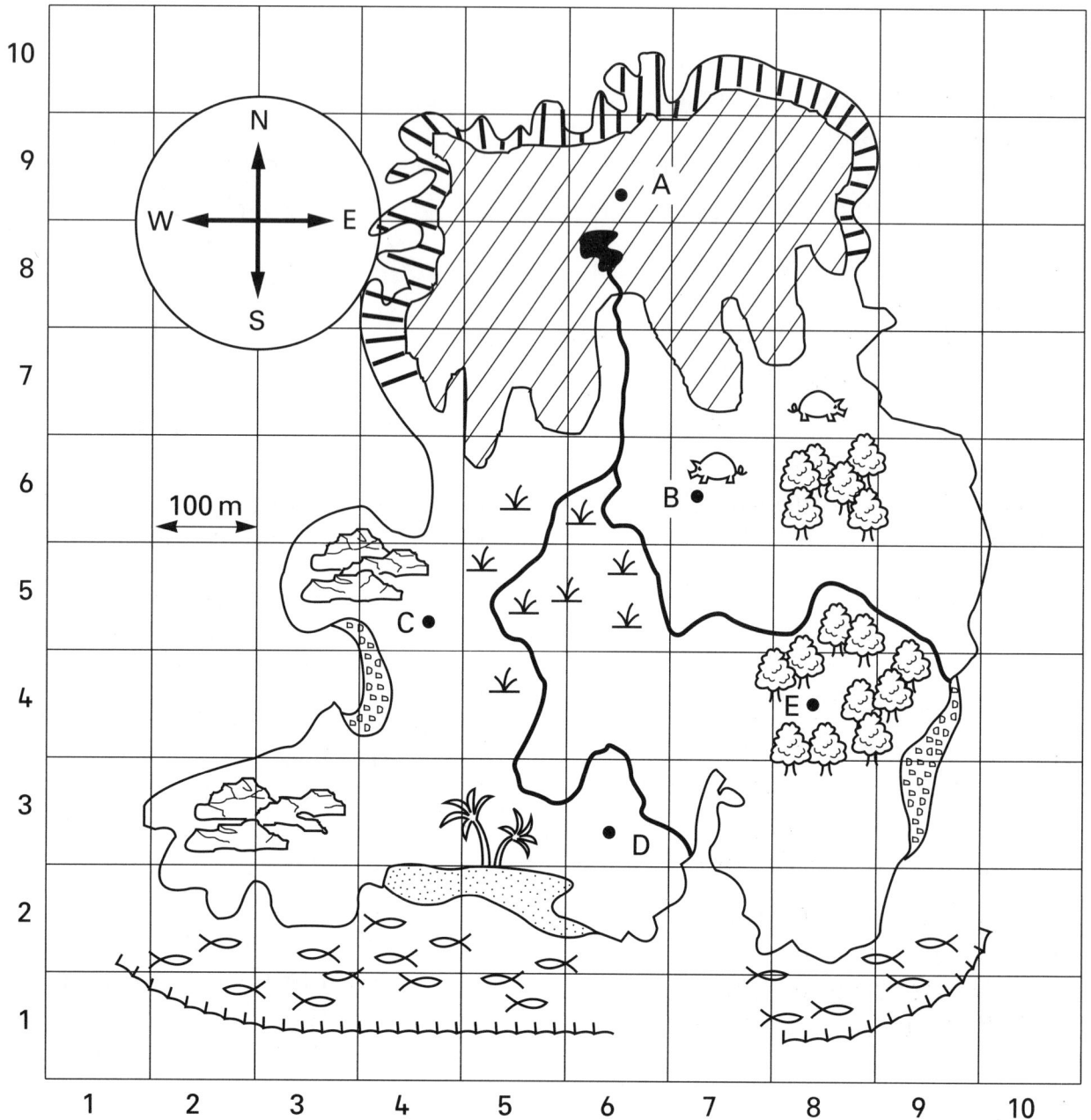

KEY

⬛ hatched	Hills
▦ dotted	Stones
▦ sand	Sand
🌀	Spring and stream

Rocks

Coral reef

Fish

Marshland

Wild pigs

Coconut palms

Woods

Cliffs

Sam's island ▷

Sailor Sam has been shipwrecked on a desert island. Look carefully at the map of the island and answer these questions.

1. Where should Sam go for a view of the whole island?

2. How wide is the island from west to east?

3. Look at the compass. Starting at A, in which direction would Sam go to:
   a) reach the cliffs
   b) find a sandy beach
   c) see the coral reef?

4. What would he see if he went to:
   a) (8,6)
   b) (3,3)
   c) (6,5)?
   (*Remember to count across and then up!*)

5. In which squares would you find:
   a) wild pigs
   b) the spring
   c) coconut palms?

6. If Sam built a raft, where could he tie it up to keep it sheltered from the wind?

7. Sam needs three things to survive on the island: food, water and shelter. How would he:
   a) get food
   b) get water to drink
   c) make a shelter?

8. Where do you think Sam should build his shelter, at A, B, C, D or E?

9. Explain why you chose this place.

Bridges 1

Write these bridge names under the correct pictures.

- Cantilever
- Arch aqueduct
- Rope bridge
- Steel arch
- Clapper
- Suspension

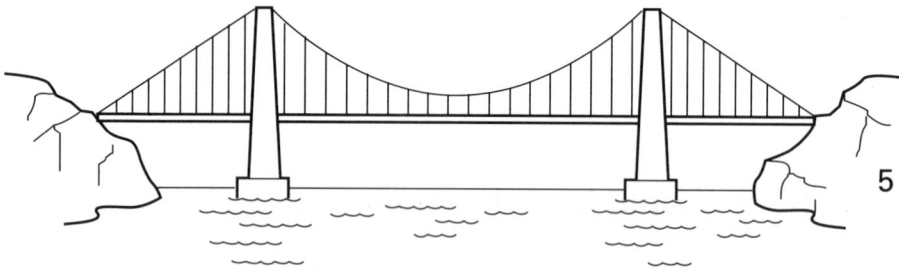

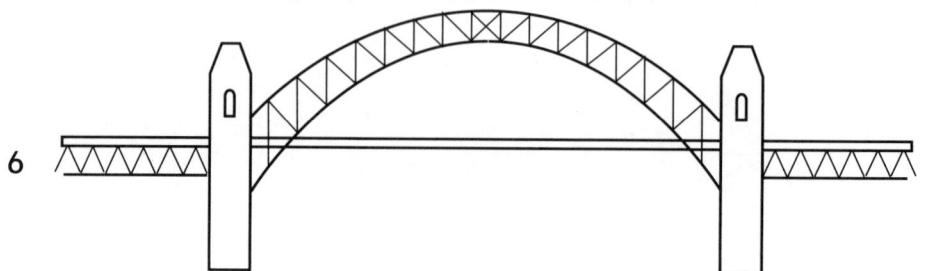

1

2

3

4

5

6

Bridges 2

Draw arrows on the bridges in coloured pencil to show the forces that act on them.

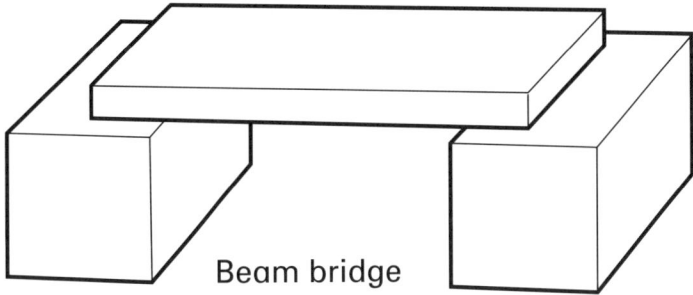
Beam bridge

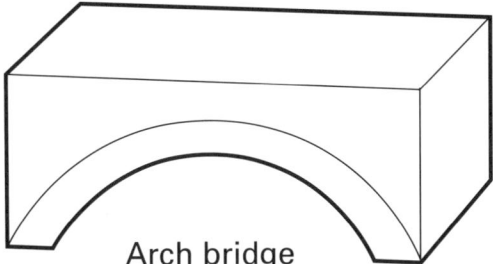
Arch bridge

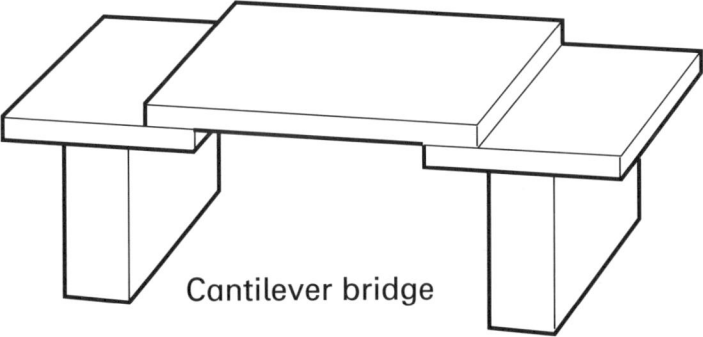
Cantilever bridge

Suspension bridge

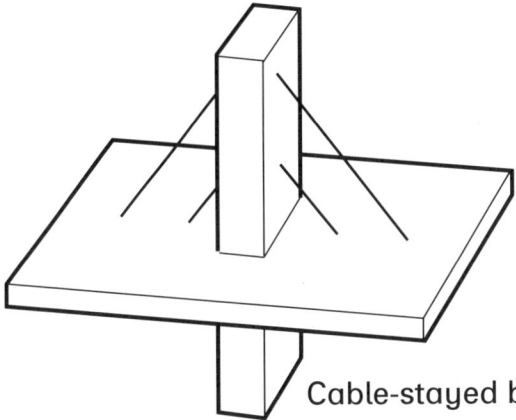
Cable-stayed bridge

Benningtown News

— 13th May —

Re-dip-velopment!

Plans to build a 1000 space car park on a site in Lower Way were under threat last night following an open meeting of the District Council.

The site, known locally as 'The Dip', has been used as a play area for the last five years while council bosses tried to decide how to use it. When plans for the car park were revealed, local people were not pleased. Last night, they handed in a petition against the development, and are pushing for the site to remain as a play area with a properly constructed playground and football pitch. Local mum, Dee Taylor explains, "Our children need somewhere safe to play, and the thought of all those extra cars in our neighbourhood terrifies me." After listening to local people's views, council members voted last night to reconsider their plans.

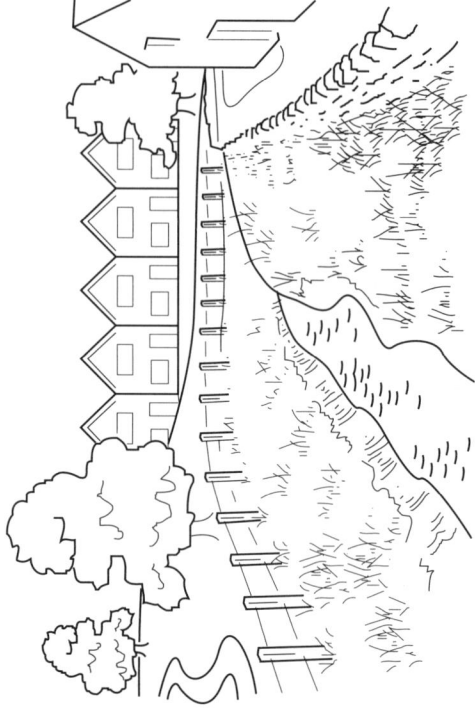

Playground apparatus

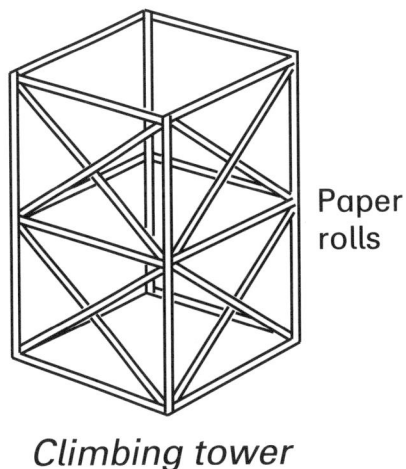

Swing

Thread or pipe cleaners

Wide lollystick

Holes made by eyelet pliers punch

Paper rolls

Climbing tower

Tunnel

Made from cardboard tubes

Slide

Dowel or a paper roll

Pipe cleaners or string

Beads

Climbing net

String

Paper rolls

Wide lollystick

Swing frame

Ladder

Made from paper rolls with pipe cleaner rungs

Describing a clay object ▷

Draw a picture of your clay object. _____

Can you tell what colour clay was used to
make the object? _____

Has the object been fired? _____

Has it been glazed? _____

What colour glazes have been used? _____

Is the object shiny or dull? _____

Is there a handle? _____

If so, how do you think it has been attached? _____

What purpose, if any, do you think the object has? _____

Where would it be found? _____

Name _____

Design and make a set of three similarly shaped Christmas decorations to hang on a Christmas tree.

This sheet should help you to design your decorations.

1. Underline four key words in the task above that show the design criteria.

2. Now, answer these questions.

   What material are you going to use to make the decorations?

   How big will they be?

   How many should there be?

   What shapes could you use?

   How are you going to make three decorations that are the same shape?

   How will they hang from the tree?

   What colour could they be?

   Do they all have to be the same colour?

Name _____

Fabrics fact file

Complete this fact file for your piece of fabric.

Colour/s: _____

_____

Pattern: _____

_____

Texture: _____

_____

This is what it looks like under
a magnifying glass

_____

_____

Other information (e.g. fraying, thickness,
water resistance, strength)

_____

_____

_____

Glue a sample of
your fabric here.

Uses of fabric:

_____

_____

User and place of use:

_____

_____

Name _____

Where do textiles come from?

Where do textiles come from?

Write whether each type of textile comes from an animal, plant or mineral.

1. cotton

2. lycra

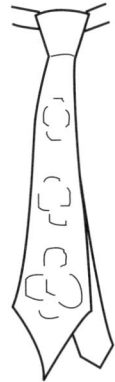

3. wool

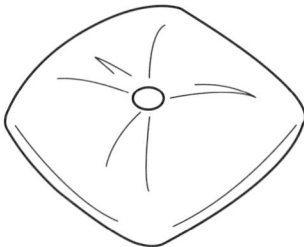

4. kapok filling

5. hessian

6. nylon

7. suede

8. silk

9. fur

10. acrylic

11. felt

14. polyester

12. rubber

13. leather

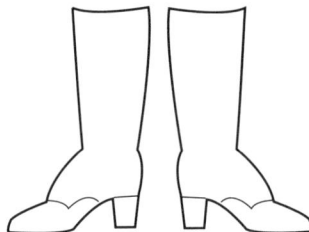

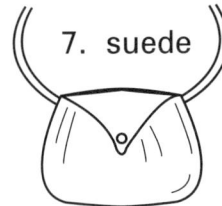

Name _____

Match each item to what it is usually made from. One pair has been done for you.

raincoat   lycra

blouse   suede

stockings   leather

socks   silk

walking boots   plastic

pyjamas   wool

swimsuit   nylon

jumper   cotton

slippers   acrylic

What are your clothes made from? Draw the label inside one of your pieces of clothing. What do the symbols on the back mean?

Basic stitches 1

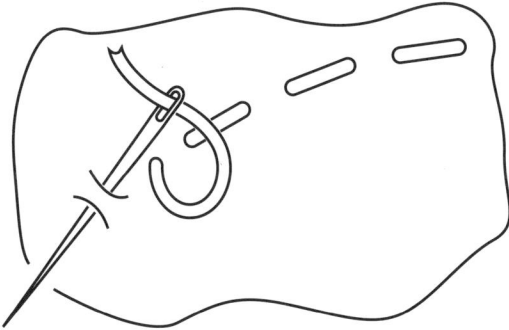

Running stitch

Pass the needle down and up through the fabric, making equal length stitches. The stitches on the back of the fabric should be shorter than those on the right side.

Laced running stitch

Running stitch can be laced with a different colour.

Use a blunt needle, and take care not to catch the fabric.

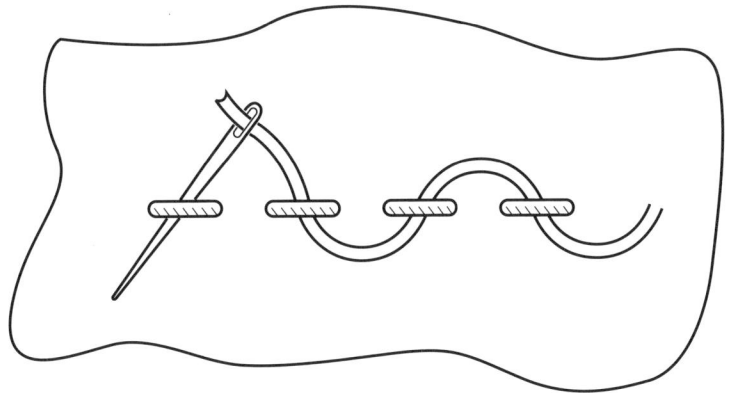

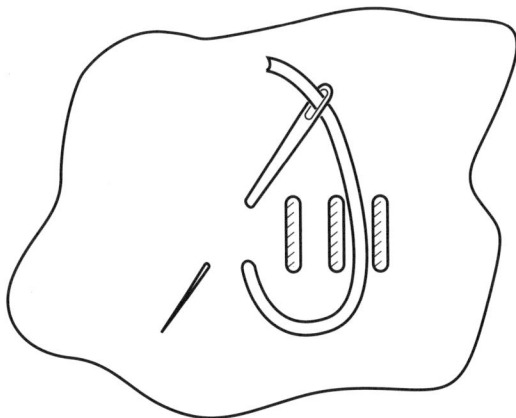

Soldier stitch

Soldier stitch may be sewn from right to left or left to right. The stitches should be equal in length with a space between each.

Basic stitches 2

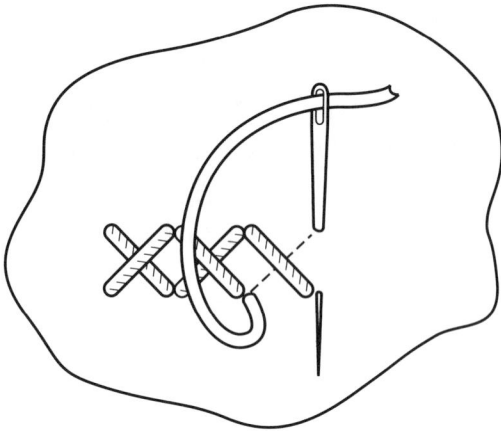

Cross stitch

Bring the needle from top left to bottom right, and complete the cross by sewing from bottom left to top right. The next stitch is made in the opposite direction.

Double cross stitch

Sew a double cross stitch by first completing one cross and then placing another over it. Each stitch should end in one corner, ready to begin the next.

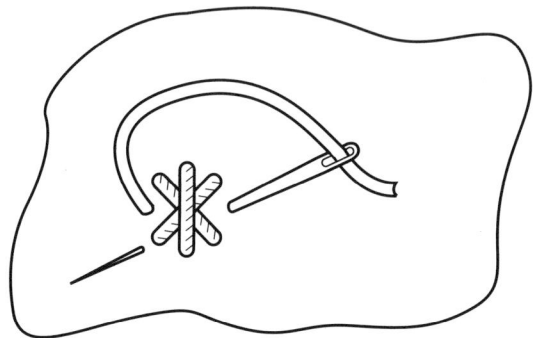

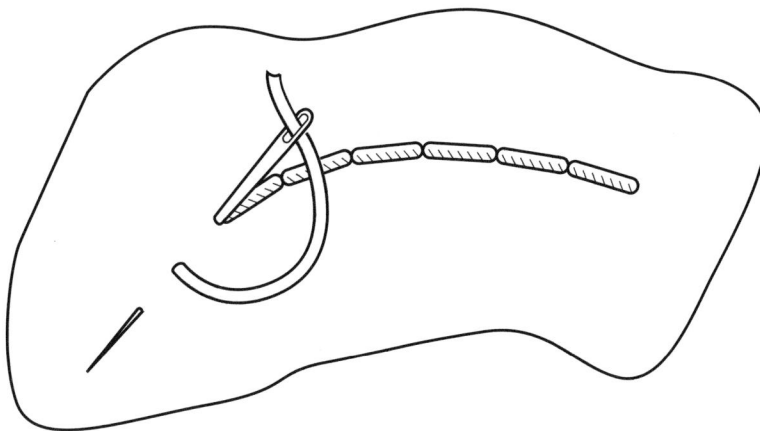

Back stitch

Position the thread on the line, and then take a small backward stitch through the fabric. Bring the needle forwards through the fabric a little way ahead, and then back and through where the stitch began.

Oversewing

Take the needle through the fabric to the back. Then bring it over the edge to the front, and push it through to the back again to produce small, even stitches. This can be sewn from left to right or right to left.

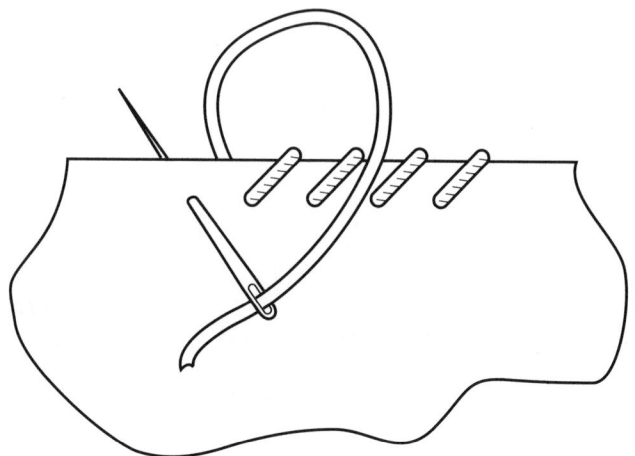

Name _____

Wall-hangings ▷

Task: To design and make a wall-hanging for your bedroom.

Here are some ideas for wall-hangings.

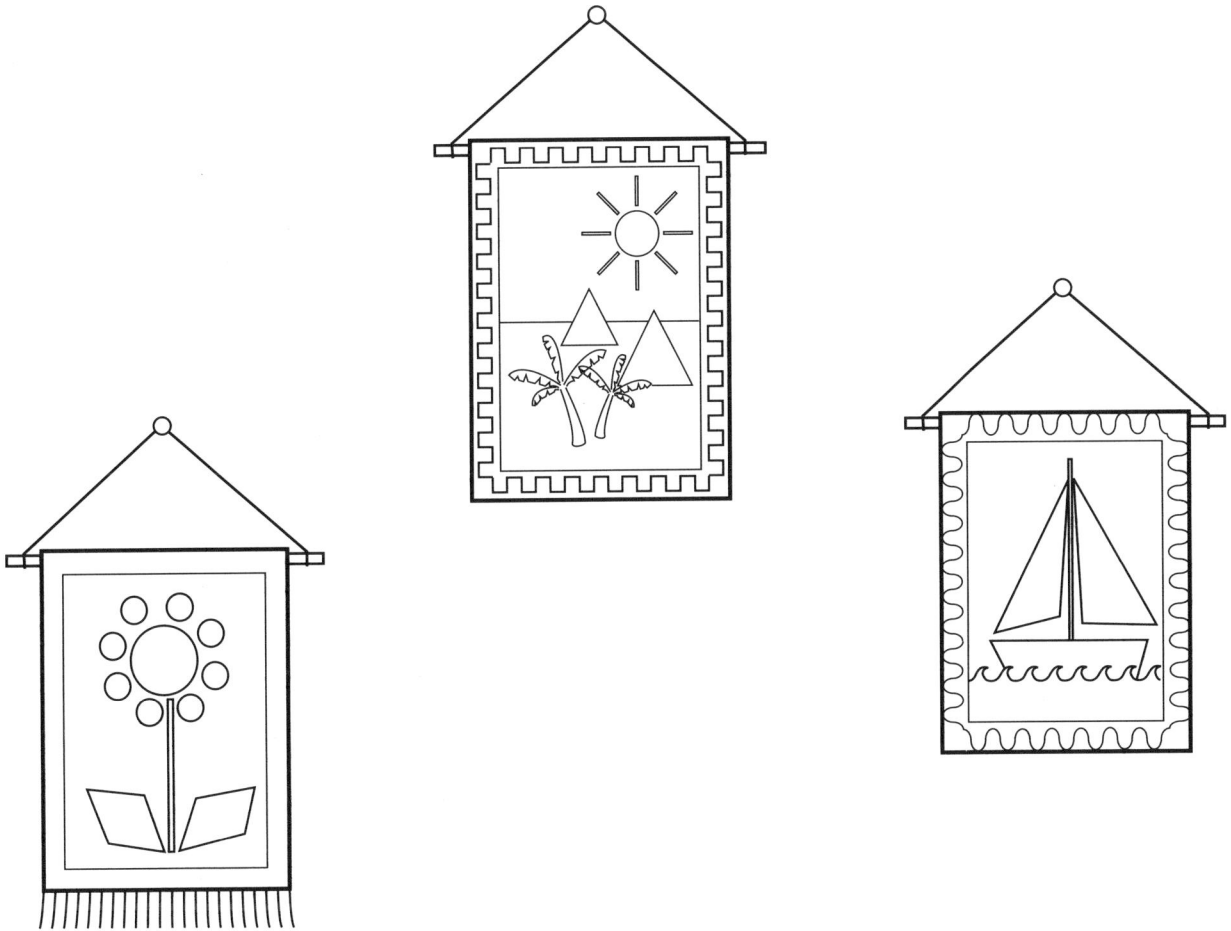

Now, try to answer these questions before starting to design your wall-hanging.

How are you going to make the border?

What shapes are you going to use for the main design?

What colours will they be?

How are you going to make your fabric shapes the right size?

How will you attach them?

What are you going to decorate the wall-hanging with?

How will you attach the dowel and string?

Containers

Answer these questions in sentences. You will also need to draw some pictures.

1. What is your container for?

2. What is it made of?

3. What is the material like? What colour is it? What does it feel like?

4. How many pieces is your container made of?

5 Look inside the container. Is it different inside?

6. How does your container close?

7. Does it have a hinge? If so, draw it.

8. What type of person do you think would use this container?

9. Where would they use it?

Now, draw your container. Use squared paper if you need to.

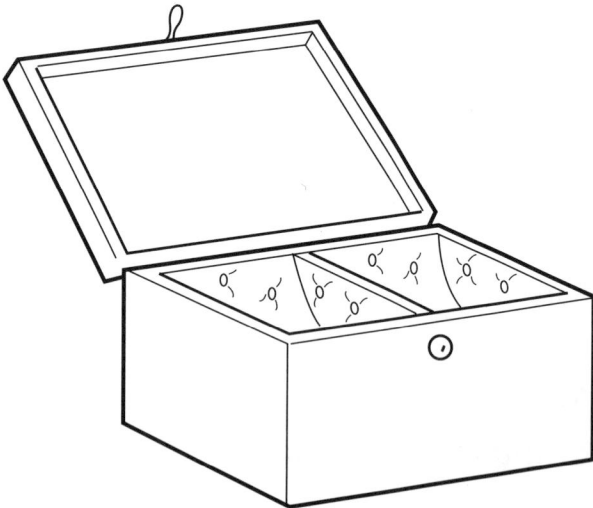

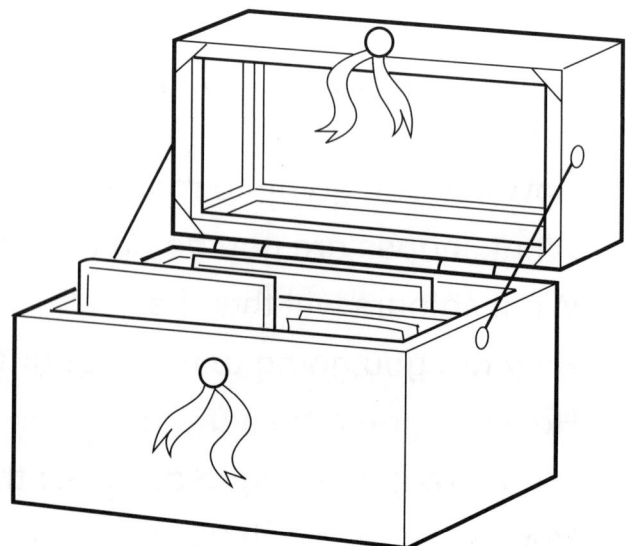

Name _____

A cube is a simple structure. If a cube is opened out, it makes a shape called a *net*.

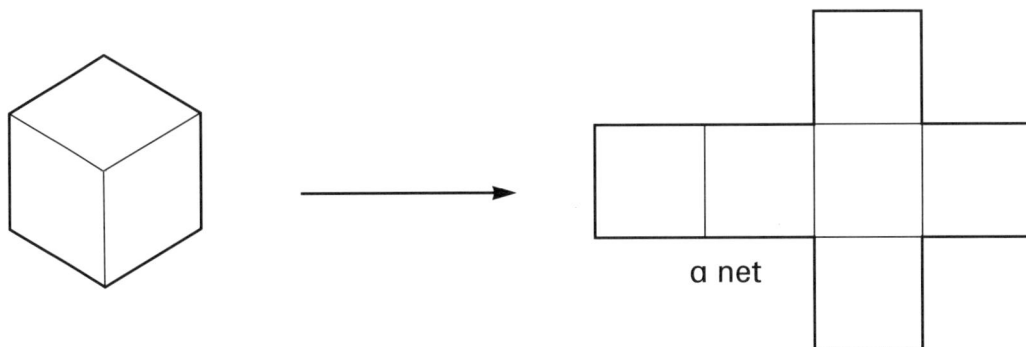

a net

Challenge: Make as many nets as you can, from 6 squares, that will construct a cube.

The squares can only join like this:

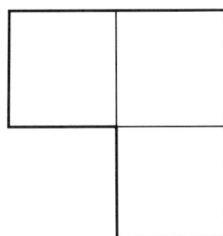

not like this: 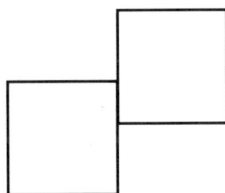   or this: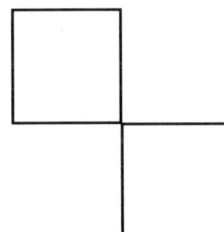

Beware, not all 6-square nets can be made into cubes!

Making a 3D frame

Step 1

Make a 2D wooden frame
15 cm × 5 cm.
Glue a large triangle to
each corner.

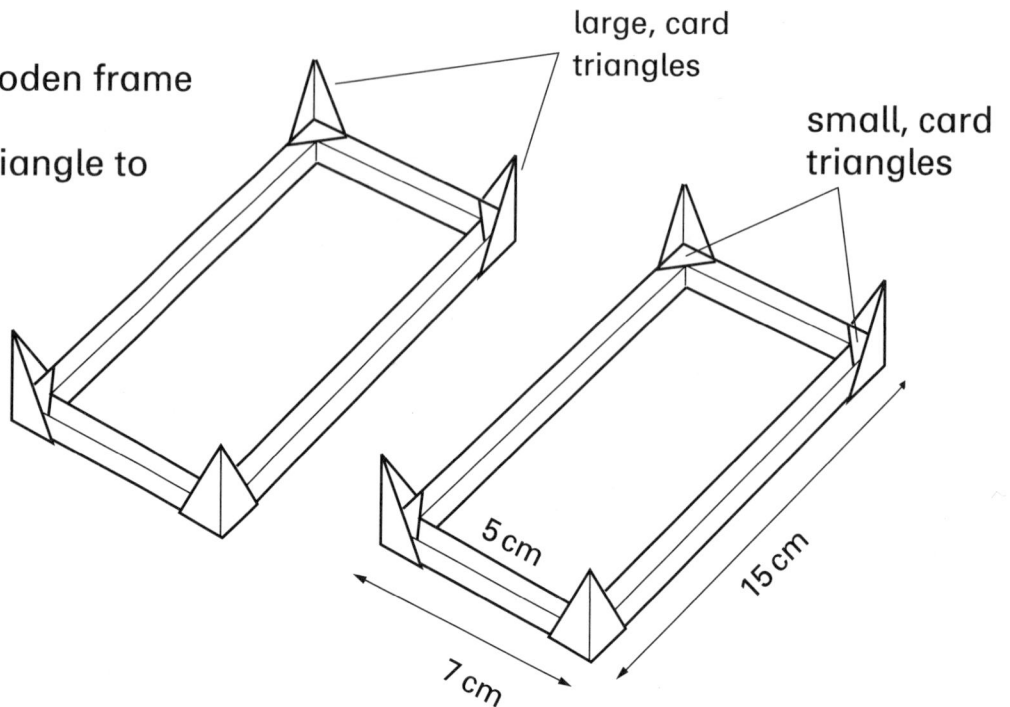

large, card
triangles

small, card
triangles

5 cm

15 cm

7 cm

Step 2

Cut 4 short lengths of wood 5 cm long.
Glue the insides of large, card triangles
and position the uprights carefully in
corners.

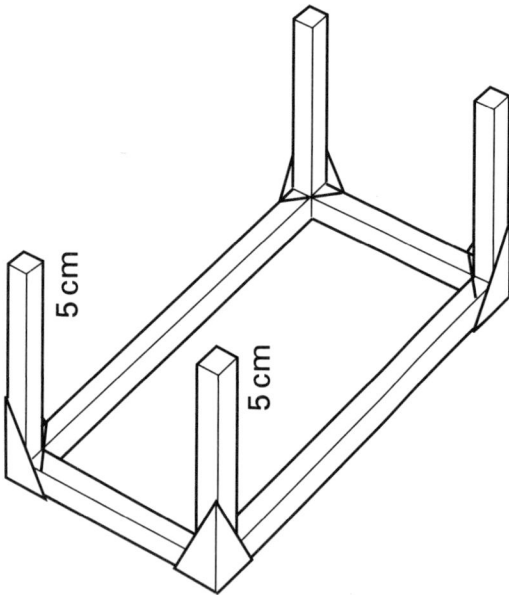

5 cm

5 cm

Step 3

Glue another 2D frame on top of
the structure using hot glue and
PVA glue.

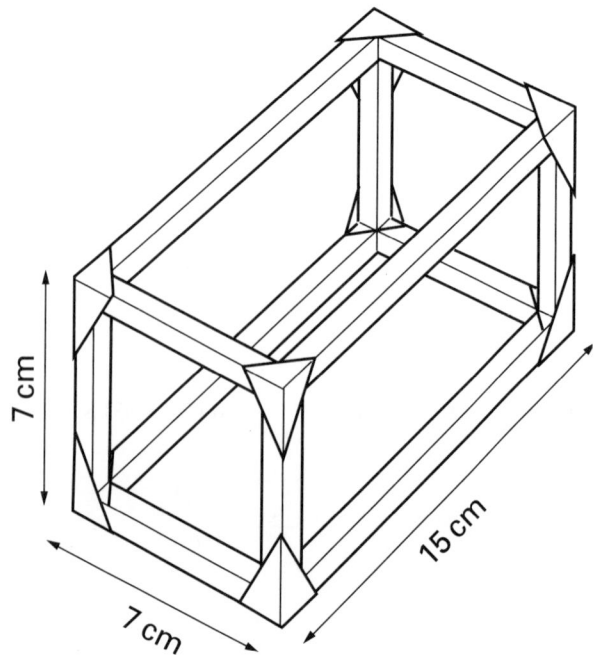

7 cm

7 cm

15 cm

Triangles for wooden frames

Centimetre-squared paper

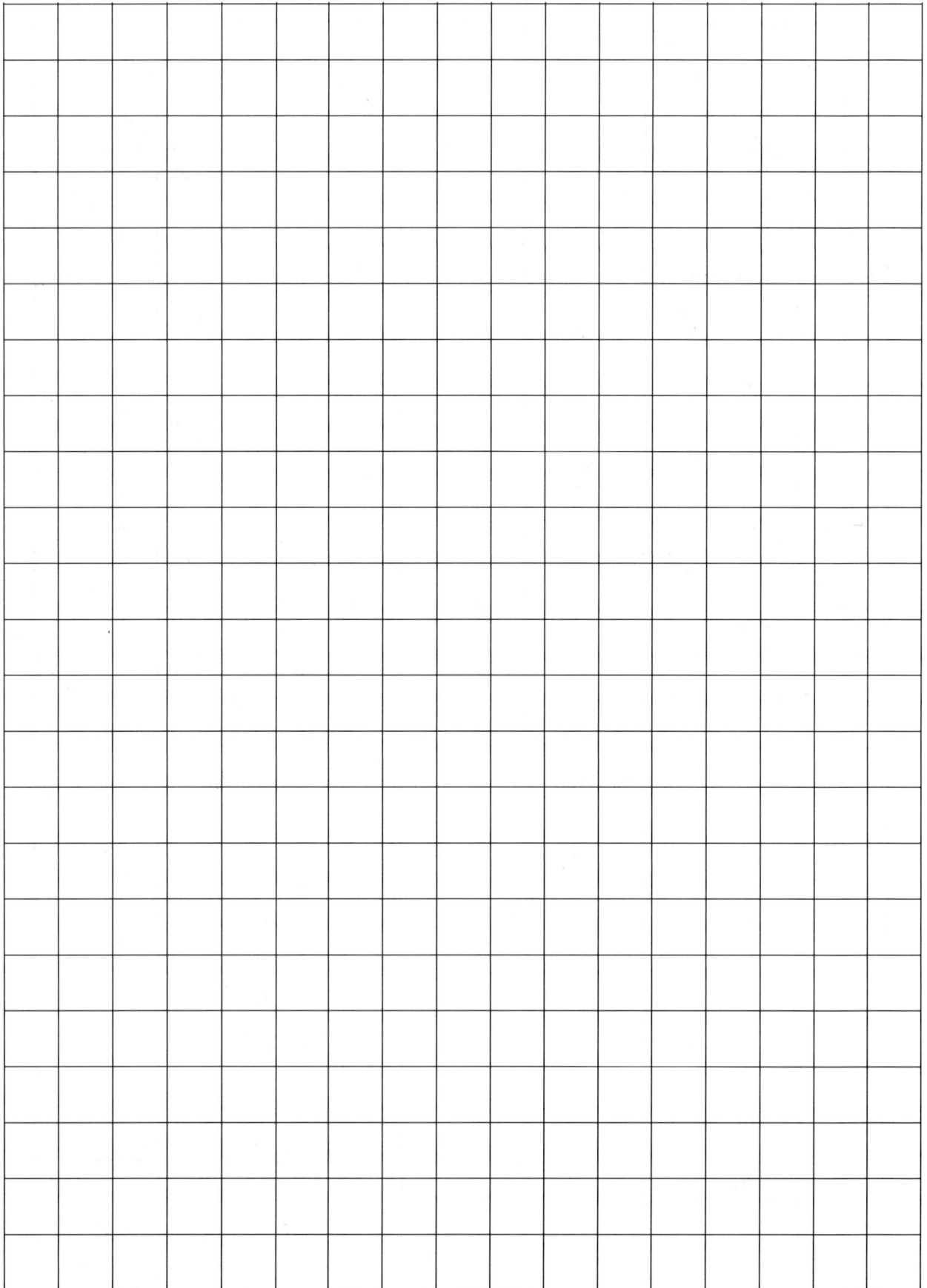

Hinges for boxes

Here are some types of hinge that are suitable for wooden-framed boxes.

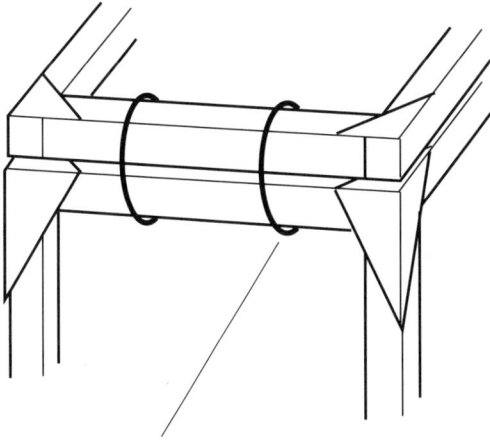

String or wire wrapped
around frame

Masking tape stuck along outside
and inside of frame makes a
strong hinge

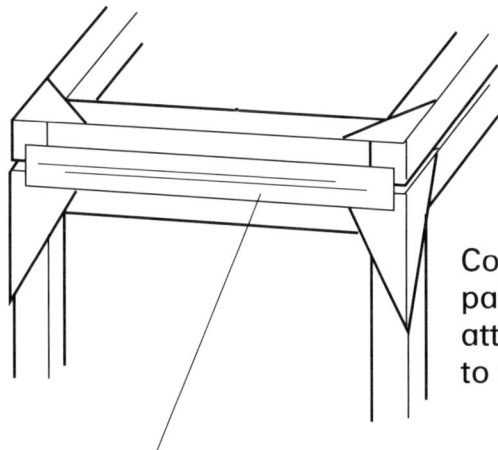

Cover or
paint after
attaching it
to the box

Masking tape

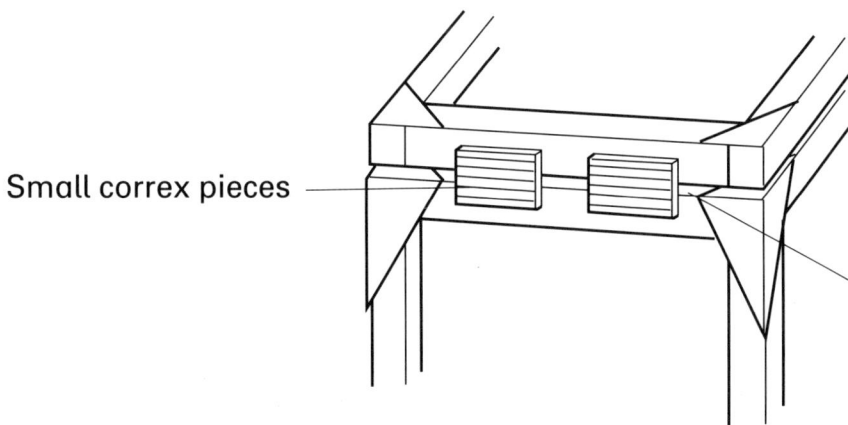

Small correx pieces

Scored along the
inside before
sticking to the
frame

Name _____

Covering a frame ▷

Step 1

Cut out some card pieces exactly the same size as the frame's sides.

Step 2

Make a paper pattern by placing the card pieces on to squared paper and drawing around them.

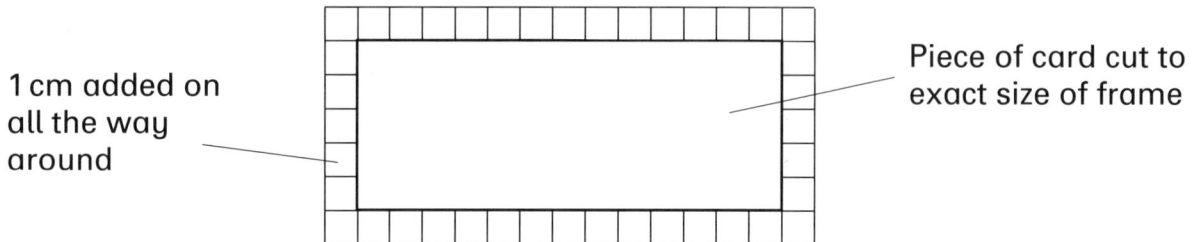

1 cm added on all the way around

Piece of card cut to exact size of frame

With a ruler add on 1 cm all the way around each piece.

Step 3

Choose a covering for your frame.

Cut out the paper patterns and attach them securely to the fabric or paper with dressmaking pins.

Cut around each one carefully and take off the patterns.

Step 4

Position the card pieces centrally on reverse side of the fabric or paper shapes.

Spread some glue thinly along edges of the card.

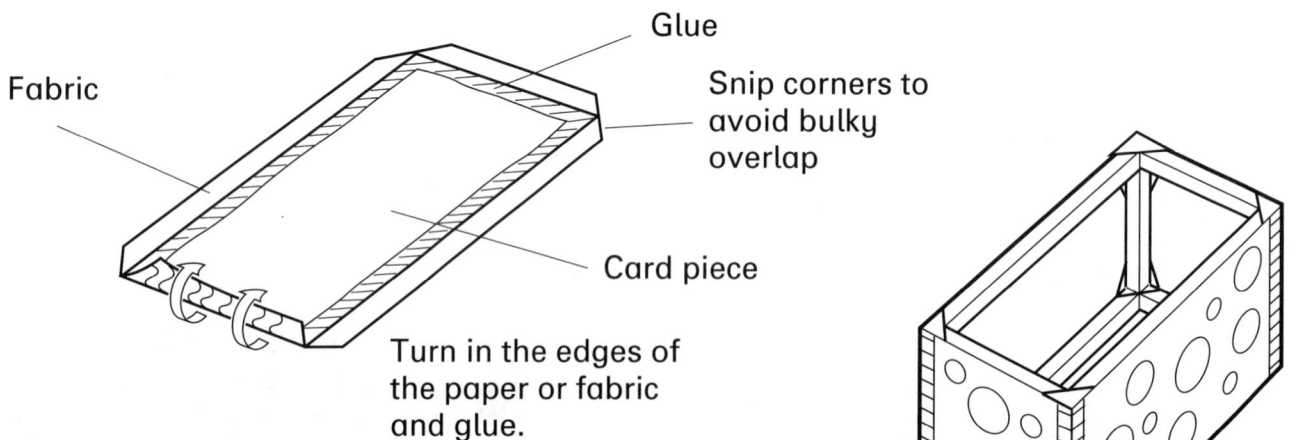

Glue

Fabric

Snip corners to avoid bulky overlap

Card piece

Turn in the edges of the paper or fabric and glue.

Step 5

Glue the covered card-pieces to the frame
Hide any joins with tape or ribbon.

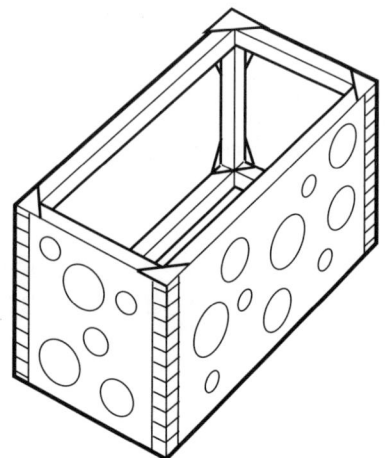

Copymaster 32

Adding a padded interior to your box

Step 1
Cut out some card pieces the same height as the frame and 2 cm narrower. The bottom piece should be 2 cm smaller all the way round.

Draw round them to make pattern pieces. Remember to add 1 cm all the way around each one.

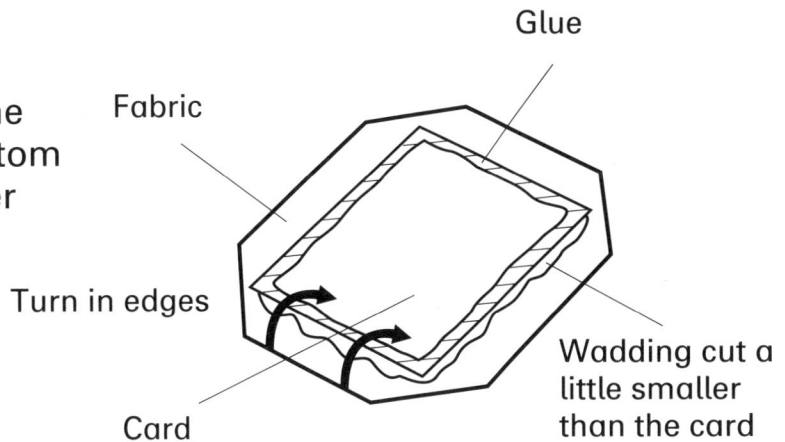

Glue

Fabric

Turn in edges

Card

Wadding cut a little smaller than the card

Step 2
Attach the pattern pieces to the fabric or paper and cut them out.

Step 3
Cut out some pieces of wadding a little smaller than the card pieces.

Step 4
Make sandwiches of fabric, wadding and card, as shown.
Glue the card edges and turn in the edges of the fabric or paper.

Step 5
Push bottom rectangle into the bottom of the box and glue.

Fabric/paper inside

Step 6
Join the other four pieces into a strip with masking tape, *fabric/paper side inwards*.

Slip this inside the frame and glue it down using PVA glue.

Card

Step 7
Cover the top edges of the box with braid or ribbon.

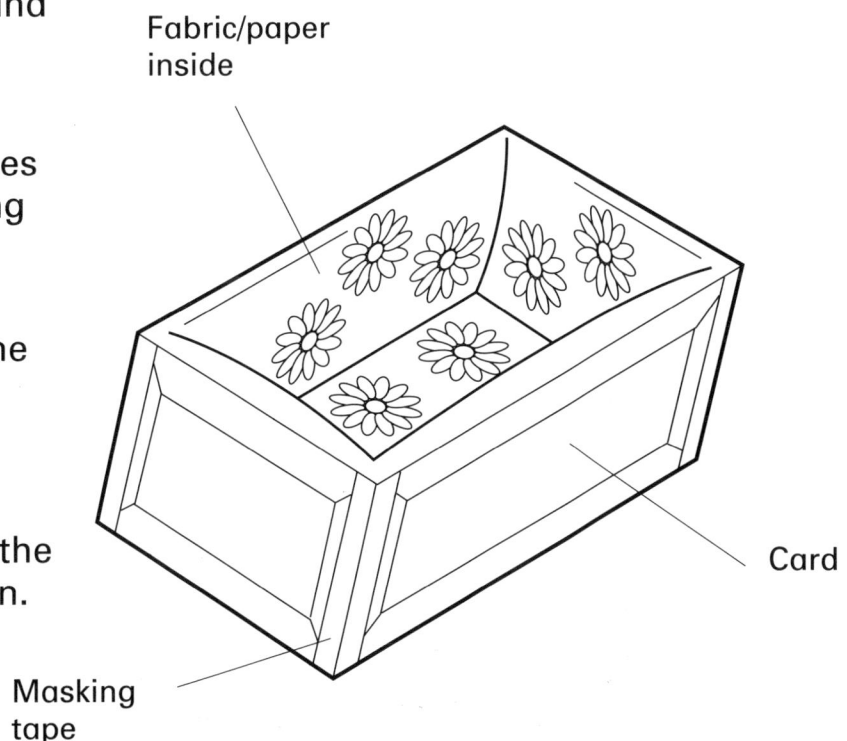

Masking tape

Name _____

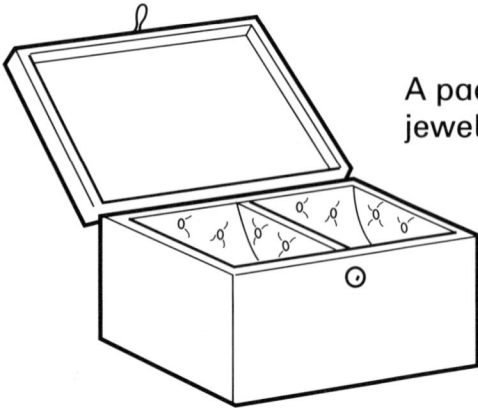

A padded
jewellery box

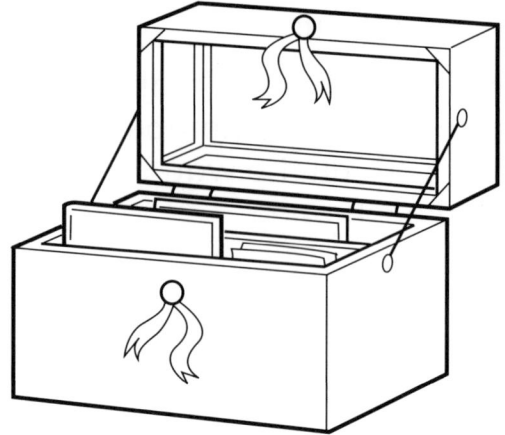

A stationery box

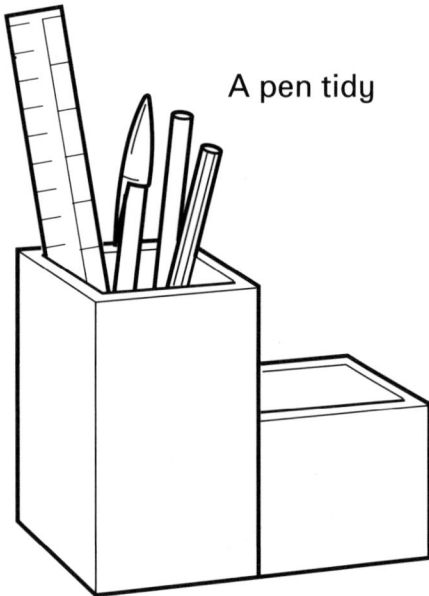

A pen tidy

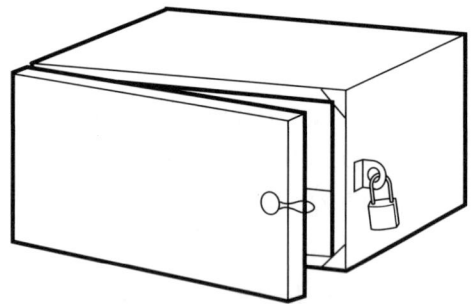

A storage box

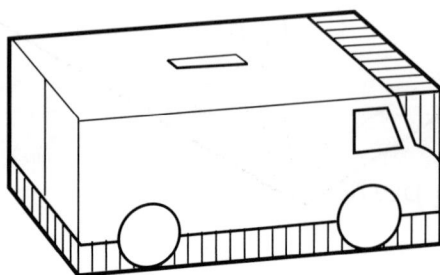

A money box

Name _____

Favourite flavours ▷

I think my favourite flavour will be:

Results of my taste test:

Taster	Favourite flavour	Second favourite
Me		

Now, answer these questions.

1. Which is your group's favourite flavour of yoghurt?

   _____

2. Which is the second most popular flavour?

   _____

3. Which flavour is the least liked?

   _____

4. Which is the overall favourite flavour in your class?

   _____

5. Write five words to describe a perfect yoghurt.

   _____

Copymaster 35

Name _____

Taste test

Flavour of yoghurt: _____

Fill in the table. Give each yoghurt marks out of 5 for each of the criteria you are investigating.

Make						Price
Criteria 1:						
Criteria 2:						
Criteria 3:						
Criteria 4:						
Total marks:						

Add up the marks for each make of yoghurt.

1. Which is the favourite make of yoghurt?

Now, write the price of each yoghurt in the last column of the table.

2. Which yoghurt is the:

   most expensive _____

   cheapest? _____

3. Which is the best value for money?

Copymaster 36

Food technology poster

FOOD
TECHNOLOGY
ONLY

NO PAINT
IN THIS
SINK

Name _____

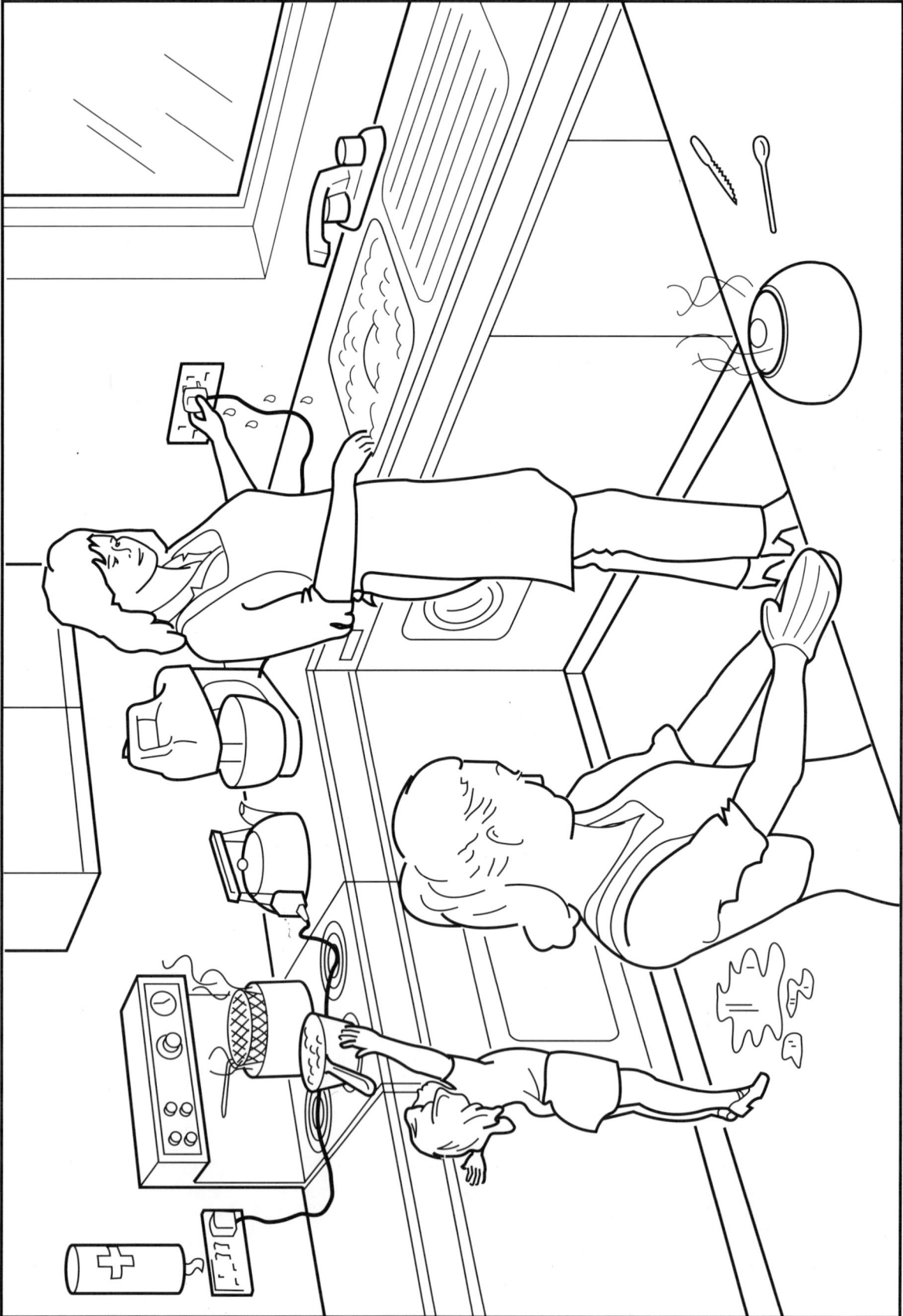

Name _____

Label these tools. Here are some words to help you:

board   pastry   mixing   measuring   dessert spoon   sieve.

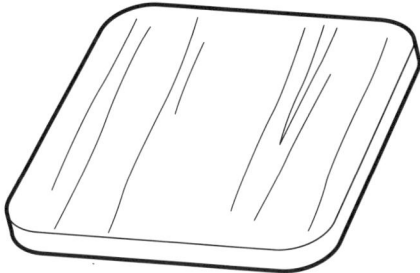

1. _____

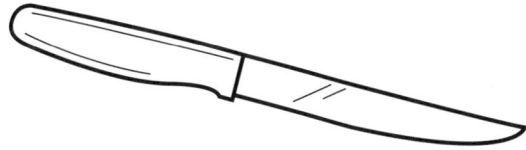

2. _____

3. _____

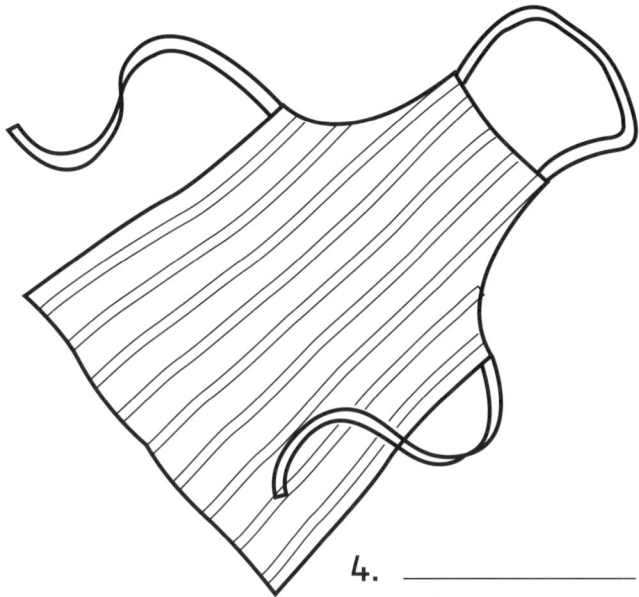

4. _____

5. _____

6. _____

7. _____

8. _____

9. _____

10. _____

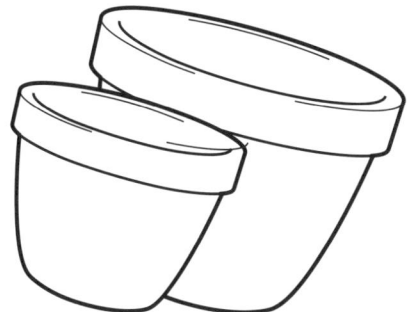

11. _____

Name _____

Cooks tools 2

Label these tools. Here are some words to help you:

whisk   palette   baking   rolling   grater   hand   cake.

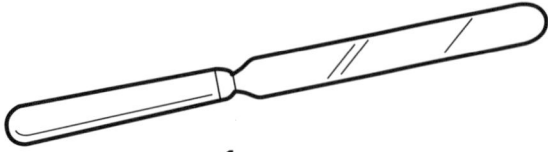

1. _____

2. _____

3. _____

4. _____

5. _____

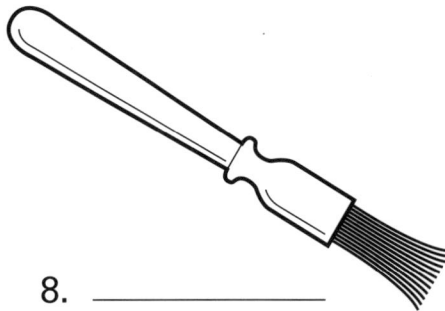

6. _____

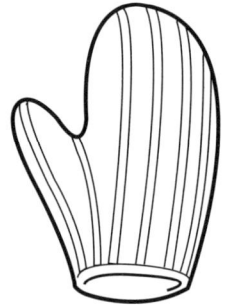

7. _____

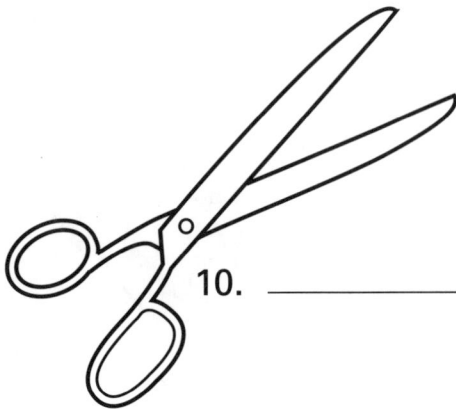

8. _____

9. _____

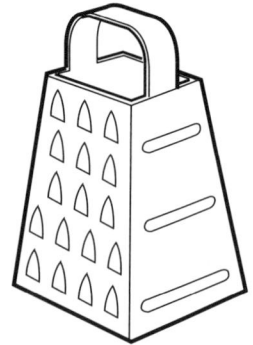

10. _____

11. _____

Name _____

Finding out about fruit ▷

Fill in this sheet for your piece of fruit.

Name of fruit: _____

Shape: _____

Skin colour: _____

Skin texture: _____

Skin thickness: _____

Edible/non-edible skin: _____

Flesh colour: _____

Picture of fruit

Number of pips/size of stone: _____

_____

Juicy/not juicy flesh _____

Picture of inside of fruit

Smell: Strong [_____] Not strong

Texture: Hard   [_____] Soft

Taste: Sweet   [_____] Sour

Usually eaten with sweet or savoury dish? _____

Usually eaten cooked or uncooked? _____

Grown on a tree or vine or bush or plant? _____

Dessert menu

Profiteroles

*feather-light puffs of pastry, filled with cream,
and topped with chocolate sauce.*

Apple pie

*traditional, crusty apple pie, served hot or cold with cream,
custard or ice-cream.*

Sticky toffee pudding

served piping hot with cream, custard or ice-cream.

Chocolate dream

*a base of light chocolate cake, covered with a layer of white
chocolate, and topped with rich, dark, chocolate cream.
A chocoholic's paradise!*

Ice-cream sundae

*a choice of strawberry, raspberry, vanilla, mint choc-chip or
rum and raisin ice-creams, or lemon and orange sorbets.*

Chunky fruit fool

Chunky fruit fool

Cheese and biscuits

Name _____

Recipe for Chunky fruit fool ▷

Ingredients:

150g fruit yoghurt

25g caster sugar

110g fruit

wafer biscuits, fruit pieces and chocolate buttons for decoration

Equipment:

small knife

chopping board

medium bowl

whisk

tablespoon

kitchen scales

serving bowls

Method:

1. Peel and chop the fruit into small pieces. Put some pieces aside for decoration.
2. Put the yoghurt into a small bowl, and whisk until thick and creamy.
3. Add sugar to the yoghurt, and whisk again.
4. Add the fruit to your mixture, and stir it in.
5. Pour the mixture into serving dishes, and decorate with the saved fruit pieces, chocolate buttons and biscuits.
6. Chill before serving.

Name _____

Kitchen silhouettes

Can you identify these kitchen tools from their silhouettes?
Label each one with the correct name.

1

2

3

4

5

6

7

8

9

10

11

12

13

14

Cooker quiz

1. Draw this cooker.

2. Write these labels in the correct places on it:

   hob
   oven
   grill
   controls
   door
   shelves.

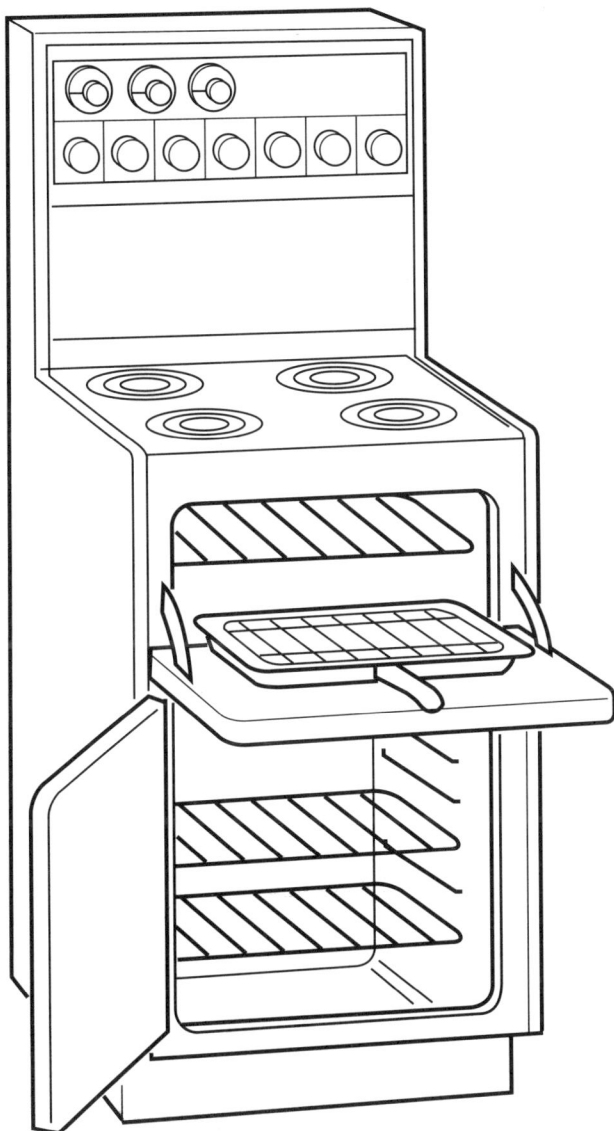

3. Now, label the diagram to show where you would cook:

   a) soup
   b) toast
   c) cakes.

4. Next, label where you would:

   a) fry
   b) boil
   c) grill
   d) roast
   e) bake.

5. Is this cooker different from yours? Draw a picture of your cooker and label the differences.

The microwave oven

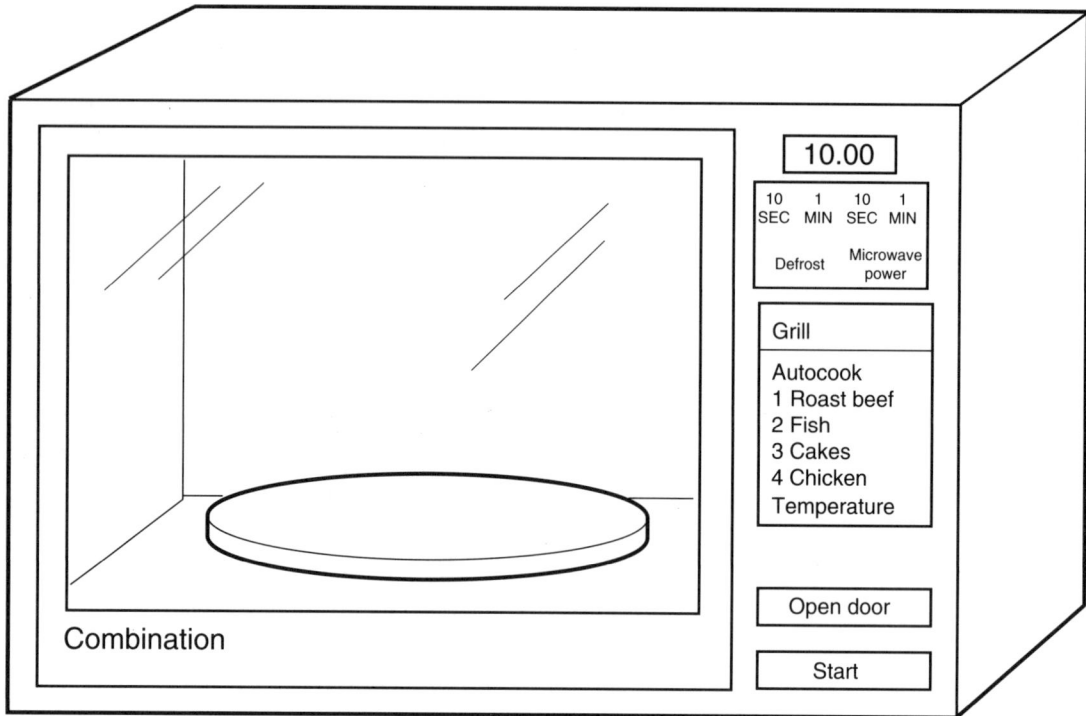

10.00

| 10 SEC | 1 MIN | 10 SEC | 1 MIN |

Defrost   Microwave power

Grill

Autocook
1 Roast beef
2 Fish
3 Cakes
4 Chicken
Temperature

Open door

Start

Combination

1. Write these labels in the correct places on the microwave oven:

   turntable
   start control
   timer
   door open button.

2. Do you have a microwave at home or school? How is it different from the one in the picture?

3. Which foods can you cook in a microwave?

4. What must you not put in the microwave?

5. If you have a microwave at home, do you use it:

   more than another oven
   less than another oven
   for different types of food?

Name _____

The refrigerator

This is the correct way to fill a fridge.

1. Label all of the different kinds of food you can see.

2. Can you think of any reasons why the foods are arranged in this way?

A fridge should always be kept at a temperature of 5° C or below. Food should be covered and stored in the correct compartment to assist hygiene and prevent contamination.

Name _____

Food hygiene ▷

Make up some food hygiene rules to go in the spaces. The words in the boxes should help you to do this.

Before you start:

1. _____

2. _____

3. _____

4. _____

5. _____

6. _____

an	wash	hair	work area
wear	back	jewellery	off
take	any	hands	your tie
cover	cuts	apron	
clean	long	the	

While you are working:

1. _____

2. _____

| up | spills | your | fingers |
| never | wipe | lick | |

After you have finished:

1. _____

2. _____

3. _____

4. _____

5. _____

floor	rinse	the	wipe	all
surfaces	cloths	cover	
the	all	wash	food	the
dishes	sweep	

Can you think of any more rules for the kitchen?

Name _____

Use this table to record everything you eat in a whole week.

	Meal 1	Snack	Meal 2	Snack	Meal 3
Monday					
Tuesday					
Wednesday					
Thursday					
Friday					
Saturday					
Sunday					

A balanced diet ▷

There are five main groups of foods that are needed for a balanced diet. They are proteins, carbohydrates, fats, vitamins and minerals.

Proteins are the main materials needed for growth, so they are often called 'body builders'. Foods that contain proteins are meat, fish, eggs, cheese, peas, nuts and pulses. Proteins give taste to a meal.

Carbohydrates are the body's energy source. They are needed to keep the body alive and active. They give plenty of calories, or kilojoules, to power the body. This food group can be divided into starches, like potatoes, pasta, bread and rice; sugars, like jam, honey, chocolate, biscuits and sweets; and fibre, such as fruit and vegetables, wholemeal flour and some cereals.

Fats are another source of energy. They are not as good for you as carbohydrates but are still necessary. There are several different types of fat, which come from either vegetable or animal sources. Generally vegetable fats are better for you than animal fats, although too much fat from any source can be bad for you. Foods that contain animal fats are cheese, butter, milk and meats. Sunflower seeds, peanuts and soya beans are good sources of vegetable fats.

Vitamins are vital for body growth and repair. Most vitamins are obtained in small quantities from foods but some people take extra vitamins in tablet form. There are different types of vitamins, and each one is named after a letter of the alphabet. Many vitamins can be found in fruit and vegetables.

Minerals are substances that are also found in small quantities in foods and have several uses. Many minerals that are required by the body, such as calcium, iron, phosphorus and potassium, can be found in our everyday foods. Calcium is important for building strong bones and healthy teeth, and iron is important for healthy blood.

In addition, it is important that we consume about three litres of water a day. About half of this is in the food we eat, but we still need to drink about $1\frac{1}{2}$ litres of milk, water or fruit juice.

Nutrition crossword

Read the clues and fill in the crossword.

Clues across
1. Proteins are the main materials needed for this.
9. Carbohydrates give you energy and keep your body alive and _____ .
11. Jam, honey, chocolate and biscuits all contain these.
12. These are the main source of energy for the body.
16. Fats from these are generally better for you than animal fats.
17. Carbohydrates are measured in calories or kilo _____ .
19. These products such as cheese, butter and milk, contain much animal fat.
20. These are vital for growth and repair.

Clues down
2. We need about three litres of this a day.
3. Minerals are eaten in small _____ from foods.
4. A baked one will be full of starch.
5. Fats are another source of this.
6. Vitamins are named after these.
7. Not very nutritious, but it keeps us going!
8. Proteins give _____ to a meal.
10. This is important for teeth and bones.
13. Proteins are often called body _____ .
14. Extra vitamins can be taken in this way.
15. Iron is needed for this to be healthy.
18. The number of food types needed for a balanced diet.

Copymaster 51

Name _____

Elements of a balanced diet

Write these names of foods in the correct bubbles. Some may go in more than one place.

bread   cheese   yoghurt   chocolate   potatoes   meat   jam   butter   crisps

fish   nuts   honey   pasta   beans   milk   fruit   cereals   rice   vegetables

PROTEINS

FATS

FIBRES

SUGARS

FIBRES

Water, minerals and vitamins are also important for a balanced diet.

Name _____

Food facts

Code these foods to show whether they contain:

□ protein ● fats △ starches ■ sugars ◇ vitamins and minerals ○ water

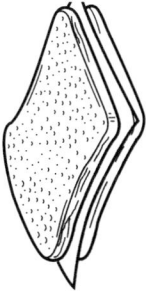   

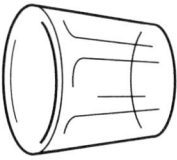 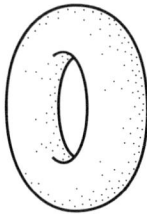  

 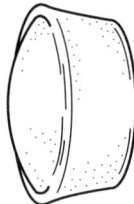  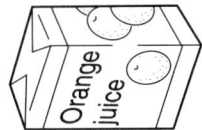

   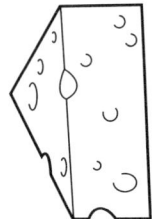

Copymaster 53

Name _____

Select some of the types of food shown on Copymaster 53 to list some healthy picnic lunches. Write or draw your menus below.

Which of the lunches would you prefer?

Pizza picnic

You and a friend are going to have a picnic. You will be making a cheese and tomato pizza as part of your lunch. Design a healthy and balanced menu that includes the pizza.

Answer these questions to help you to design your menu.

What nutritional elements does pizza contain?

What other elements will you need to make a balanced meal?

What foods contain these elements?

How much of each food will you need?

How will you carry your picnic?

Will you need anything else for your picnic?

Scone-based pizza

Equipment

scales

medium-sized bowl

small bowl

sieve

fork

plastic mixing spoon or
wooden spoon

rolling-pin

baking sheet

small saucepan

sharp knife

chopping board

grater

measuring jug

Ingredients

For the scone base:

200 g self-raising flour

50 g margarine

$\frac{1}{2}$ teaspoon of salt

150 ml of milk

For the topping:

3–4 tablespoons of tinned
tomatoes

1 teaspoon of cornflour

75 g grated cheese

1 small onion – chopped

$\frac{1}{2}$ teaspoon of sugar

salt

pepper

mixed herbs

Name _____

Method for making scone-based pizza ▷

1. Grease a baking sheet and set the oven at 200° C.

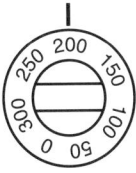

2. Sieve the flour and 1/2 teaspoon of salt into a medium-sized mixing bowl.

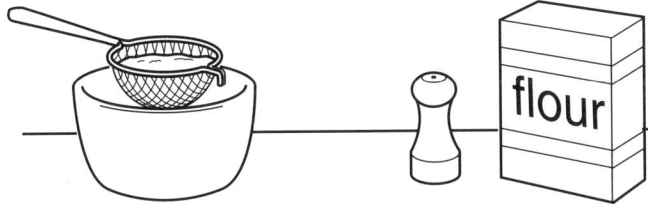

flour

3. Using a fork and then your fingertips, press the margarine and flour together until the mixture looks like fine breadcrumbs.

4. Add the milk gradually, and mix into a soft

5. Roll out the dough into a small circle, and place it on a baking tray.

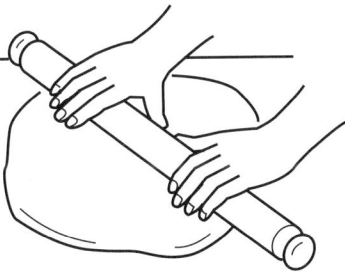

6. Place the tomatoes in a saucepan and blend in the cornflour. Bring the mixture to the boil until it thickens.

7. Add in salt, pepper and sugar. Then allow the mixture to cool.

8. Place the tomato mixture, chopped onion and grated cheese on the dough base. Sprinkle the mixed herbs on top.

9. Bake the pizza for 20 minutes until golden brown.

20:00

Name _____

Picnic design

□ protein ● fats △ starches ■ sugars ◇ vitamins and minerals ○ water

These are different foods I will eat

Pizza

Shopping list

Lighting up history

Here are some pictures of lamps from different historical periods.
Cut out the pictures and put them in order to make a 'light timeline'.

Egyptian pottery
lamp

Firelight

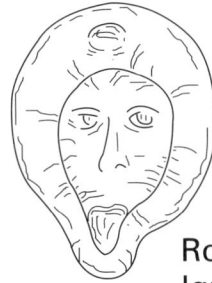

Roman oil
lamp

1950s utility light

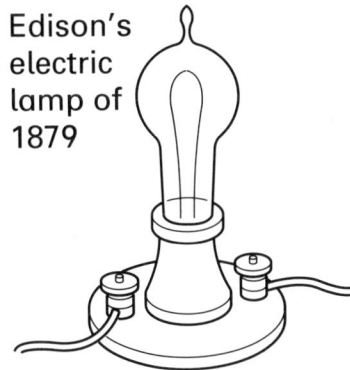

Edison's
electric
lamp of
1879

Modern 'high
tech' lamp

18th-
century
beeswax
candle

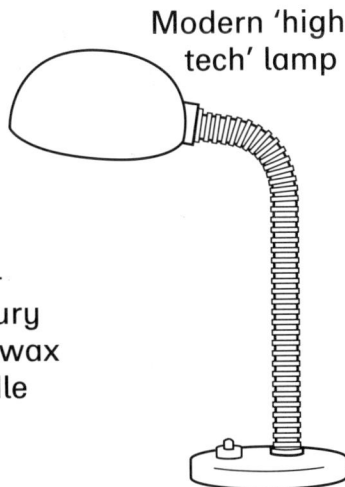

1920s Art Deco lamp

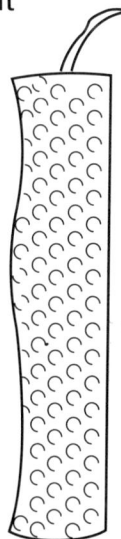

Late-Victorian paraffin lamp

Name _____

Write these labels in the correct places on the picture:

battery
bulb
switch
reflector
spring

Now, answer these questions.

1. What happens when the switch is moved in the direction of the arrow?

2. What is the spring for?

3. What is the reflector for?

Copymaster 60

Electricity identity kit

Check your electricity kit by placing each component on top of its picture.

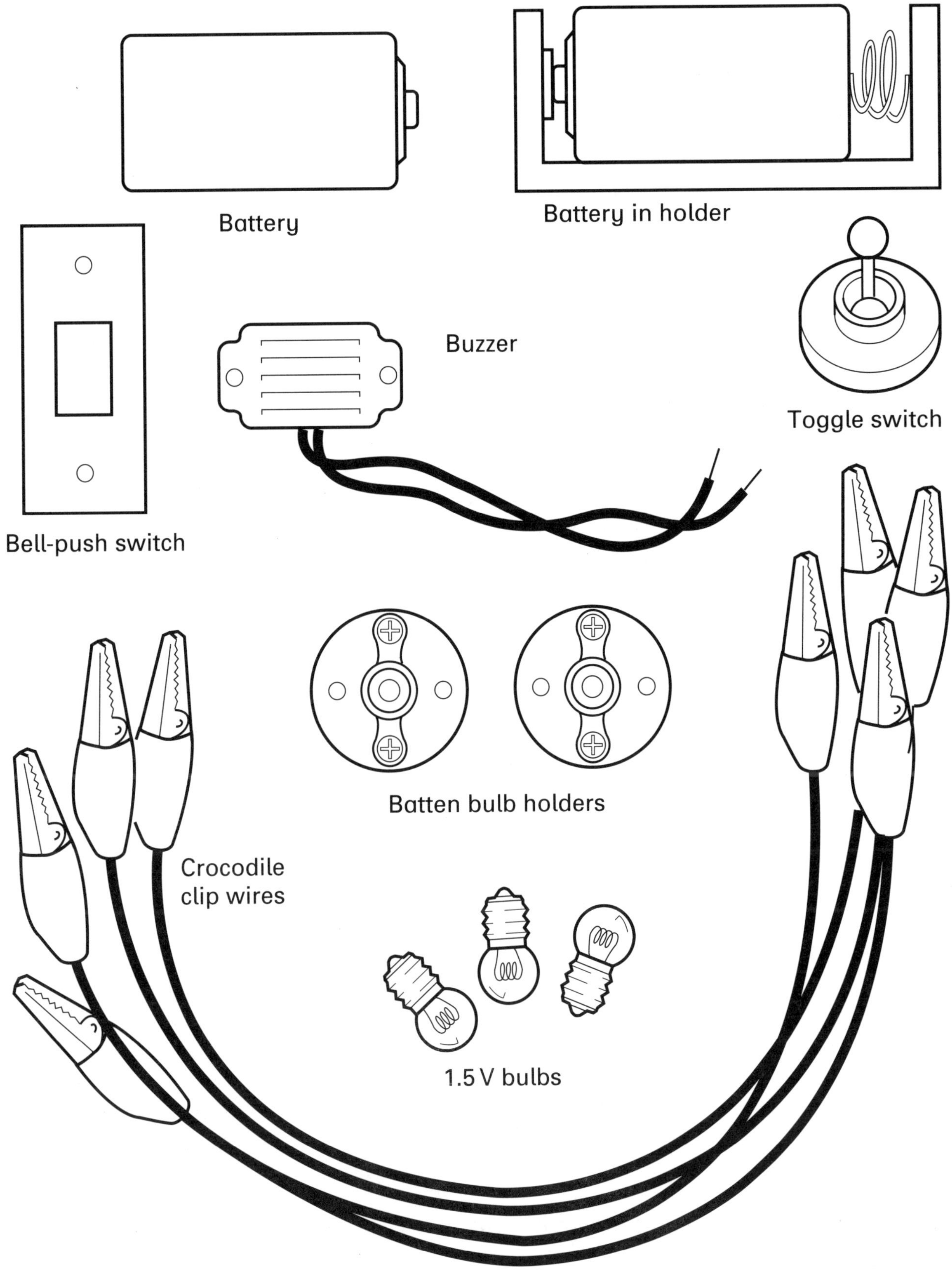

Battery

Battery in holder

Bell-push switch

Buzzer

Toggle switch

Batten bulb holders

Crocodile clip wires

1.5 V bulbs

Name _____

When your circuit doesn't work....

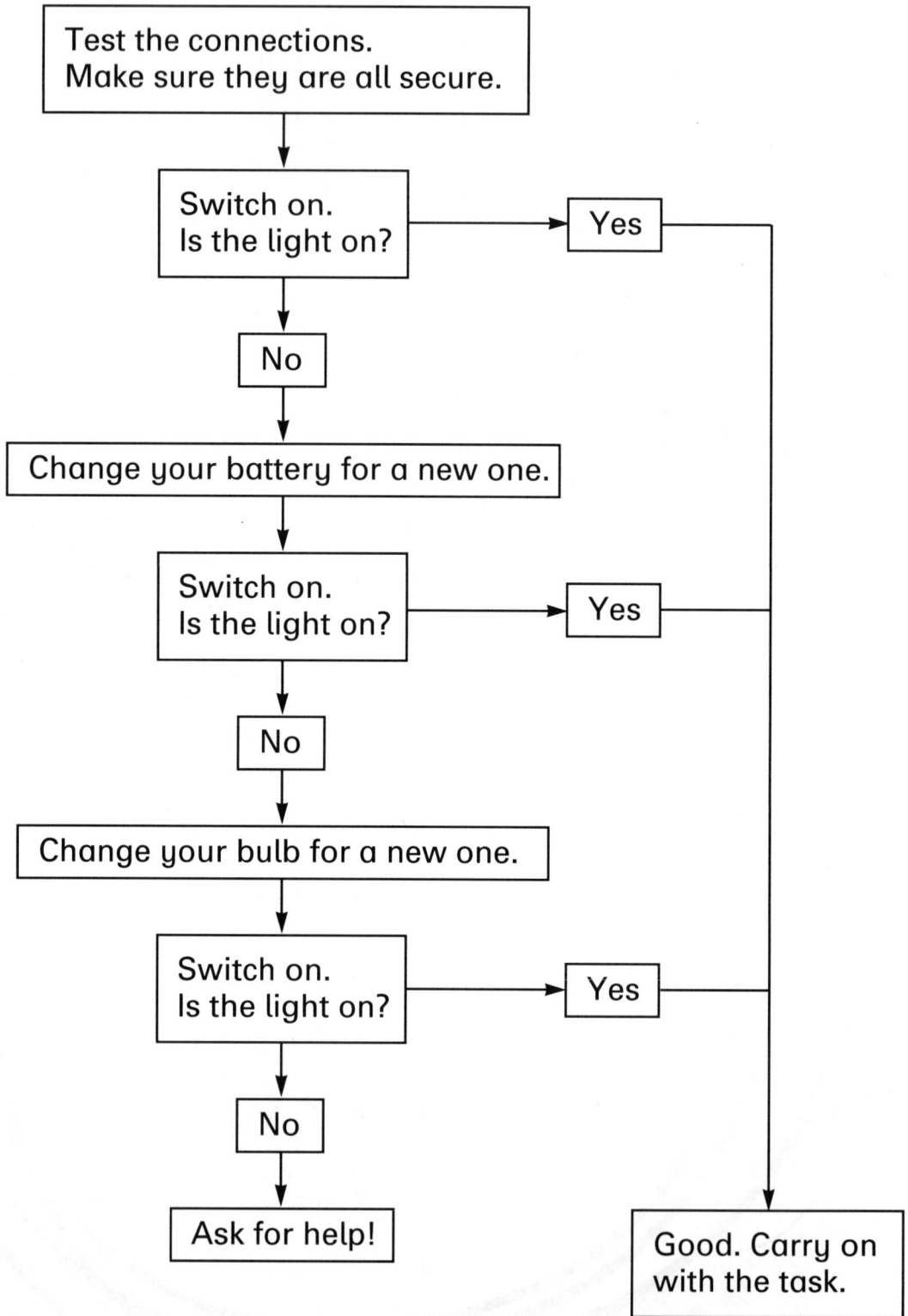

Test the connections.
Make sure they are all secure.

↓

Switch on.
Is the light on? → Yes

↓

No

↓

Change your battery for a new one.

↓

Switch on.
Is the light on? → Yes

↓

No

↓

Change your bulb for a new one.

↓

Switch on.
Is the light on? → Yes

↓

No

↓

Ask for help!

Good. Carry on with the task.

When you have got your basic circuit to work, test the other components one by one.

Copymaster 62

Name _____

Electricity identity parade ▷

Label the electrical components correctly. These words should help you:

bell-push   buzzer   battery   reed   toggle   crocodile   switch   holder.

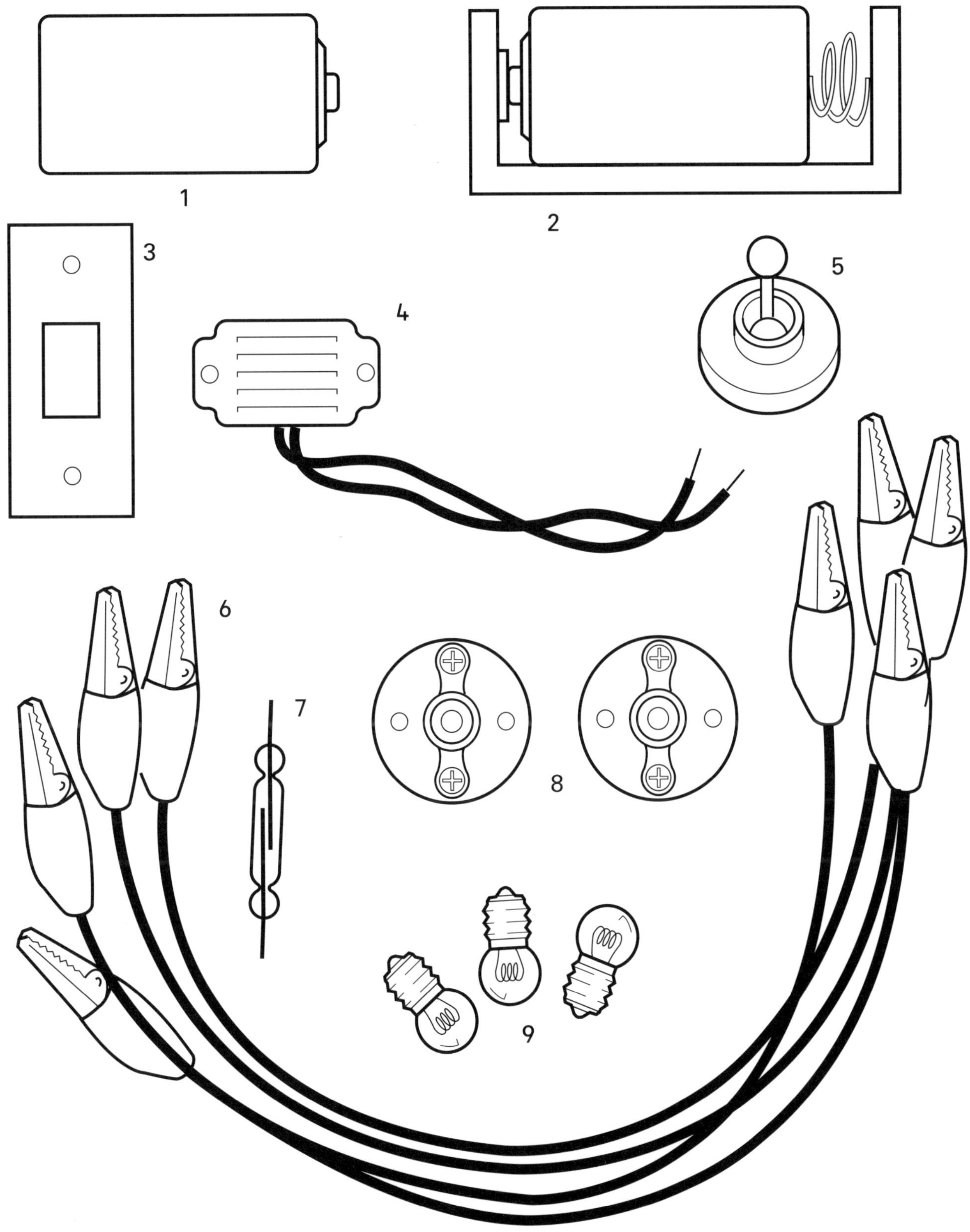

1

2

3

4

5

6

7

8

9

Michael Faraday (1791–1867) ▷

Michael Faraday was one of the greatest of British experimental physicists. He taught himself science from an encyclopedia before starting to work for a well-known chemist, Humphry Davy. At this time, scientists were just learning how to produce electricity and Faraday's work helped them greatly. In 1831, he discovered how to generate electricity, but it was a long time before electricity was used in the home. The earliest electric cookers were not produced until 1879, twelve years after his death.

Michael Faraday's experiments provided the basis for the electric motor, which is used in many of our household appliances, such as washing machines, hi-fi systems, cameras and freezers.

The most common ways of making electricity nowadays involve converting chemical energy into electrical energy, either through a chemical reaction, as in a battery, or by burning fuels such as coal and gas.

Answer the following questions in sentences.

1. When did Michael Faraday live?

2. How did he first learn science?

3. When did Faraday learn how to generate electricity?

4. How old was he at that time?

5. Which fuels are commonly burnt to produce electricity?

Make a list of all the electrical appliances that you can think of in your home.

Name _____

Switching on

Label each diagram to show how the switch works.

Toggle switch

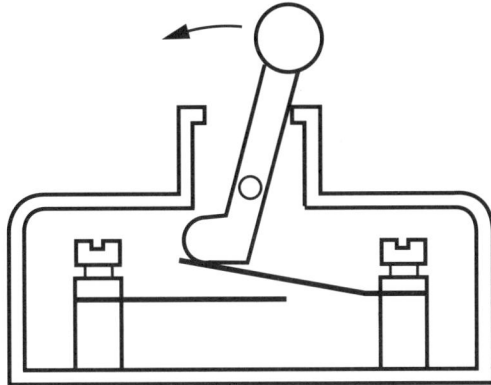

Bell-push switch

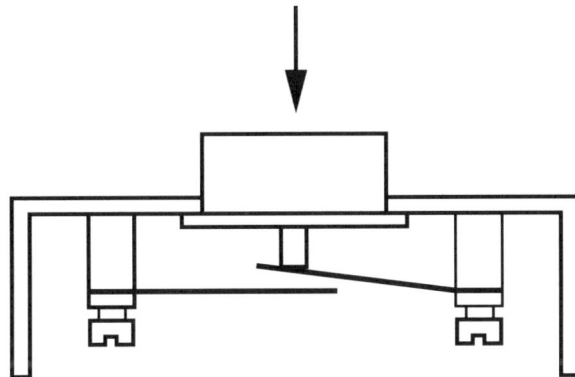

Reed switch

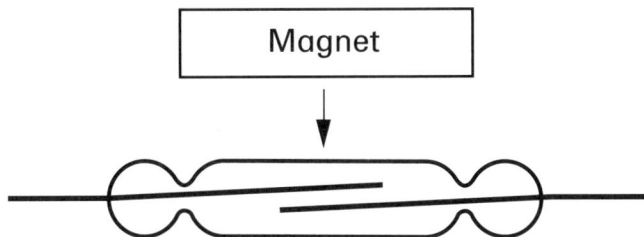

Magnet

Traffic lights

Green

Amber

Red

Complete this circuit diagram to make the three bulbs light in turn.

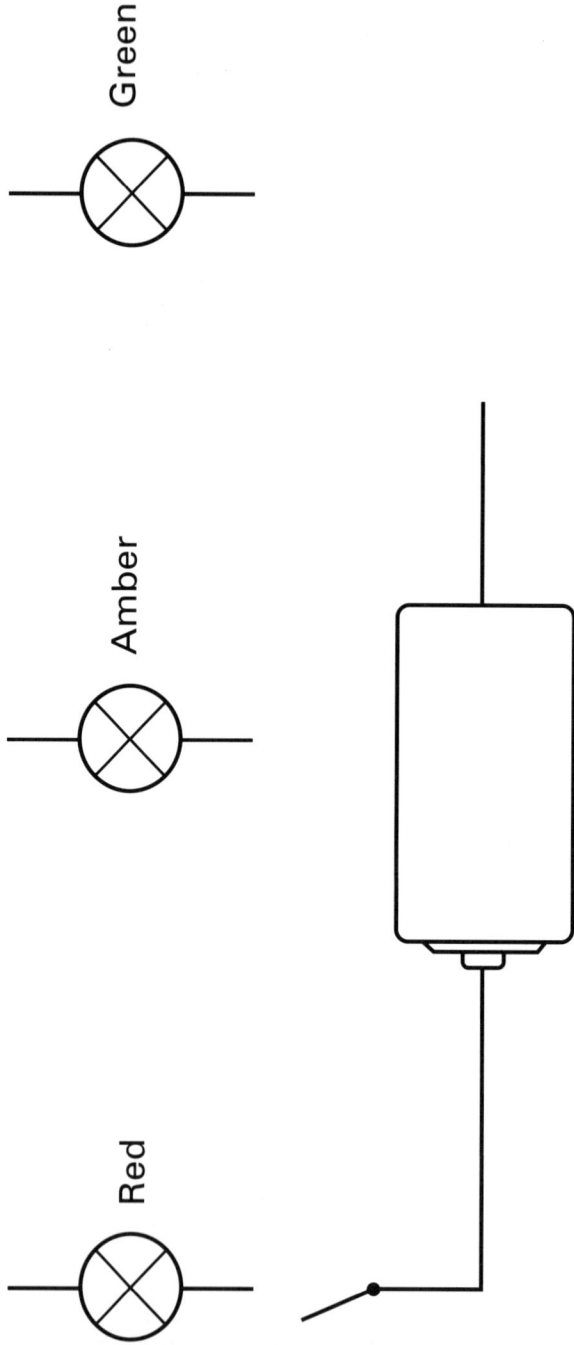

Identifying levers

A lever is a rigid bar which moves around a pivot or fulcrum.

Look carefully at each lever. Colour the lever red and the pivot blue.

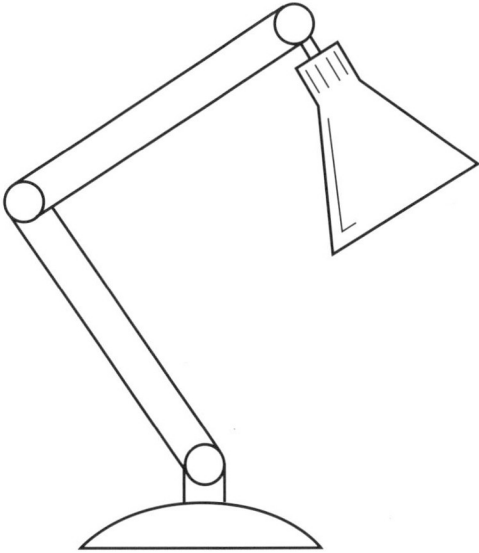

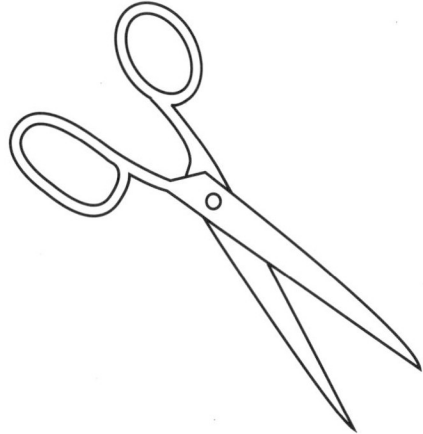

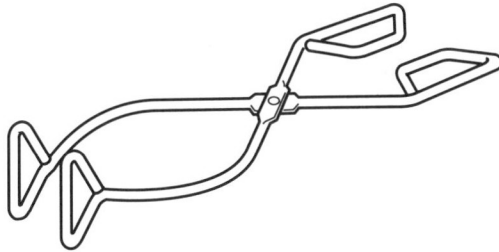

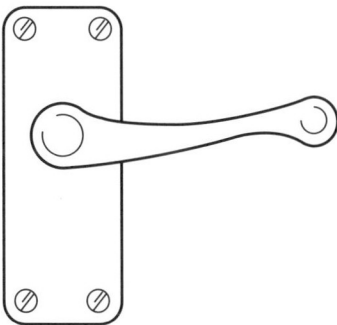

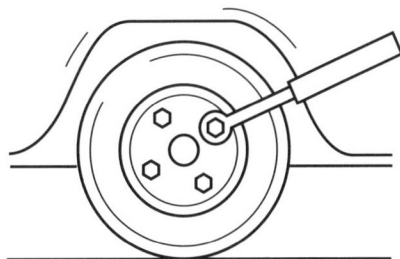

Design a toy

Woodall & Caldecott Publishers Ltd. are planning to publish a series of children's books. They want to create a set of toys to be sold alongside the new titles.

Task: To design and make a prototype for a moving puppet that is linked to a character from a children's book.

Name _____

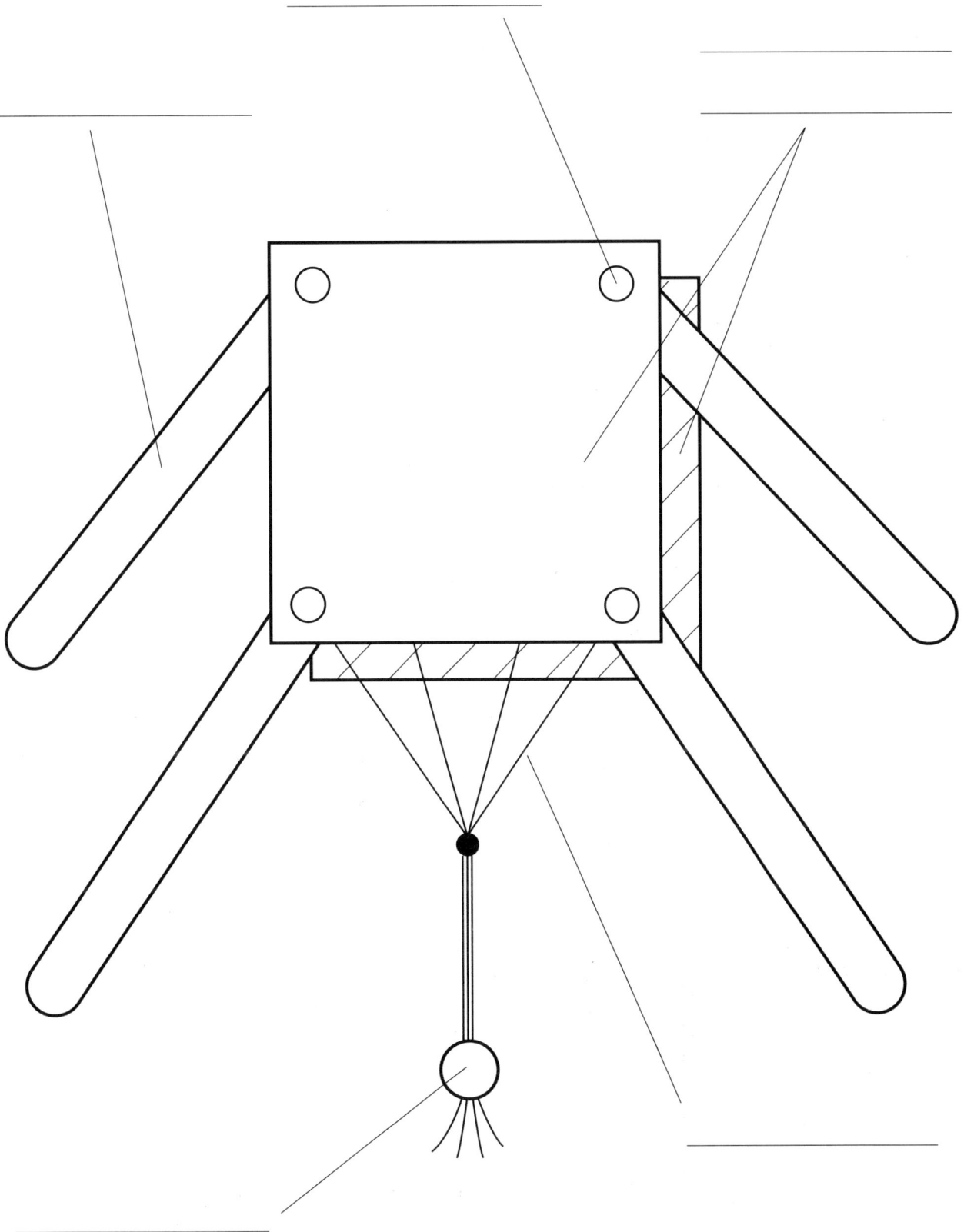

Name _____

Balance each seesaw by adding one weight. Then complete the sums correctly.

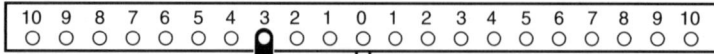
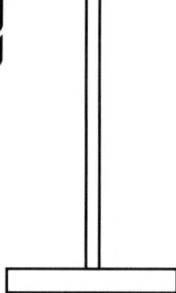

$2 \times 3 =$

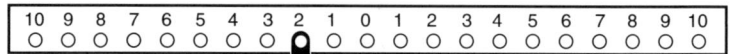
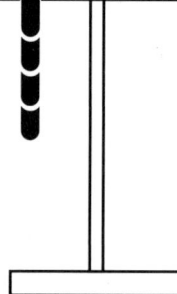

$4 \times 2 =$

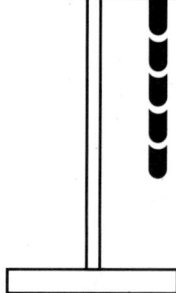

$= 5 \times 2$

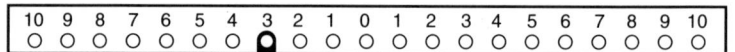

$3 \times 3 =$

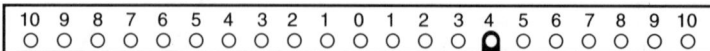
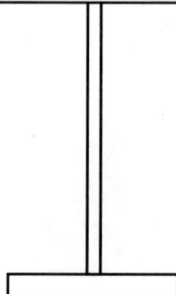

$= 2 \times 4$

Remember, a longer lever needs less effort to lift a weight.

Copymaster 70

Levers 2

On each of these pictures, label the pivot and draw arrows to show where the effort is applied. The first one has been done for you.

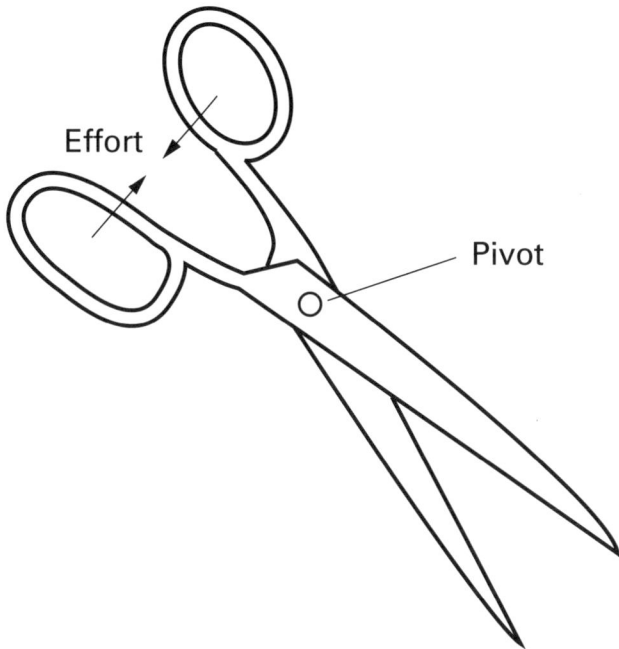

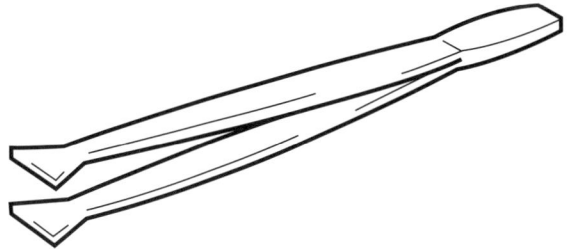

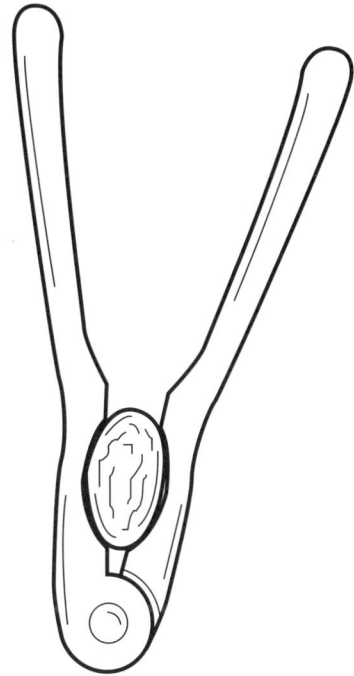

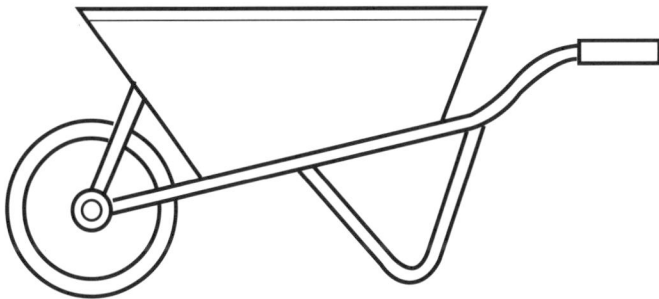

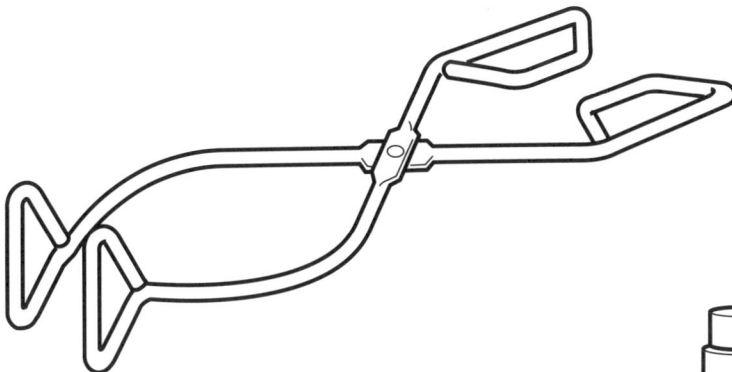

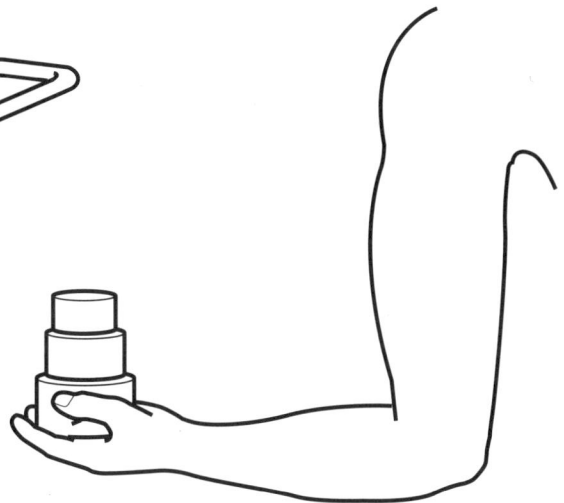

Effort

Pivot

Write if each object is a first-, second- or third-class lever.

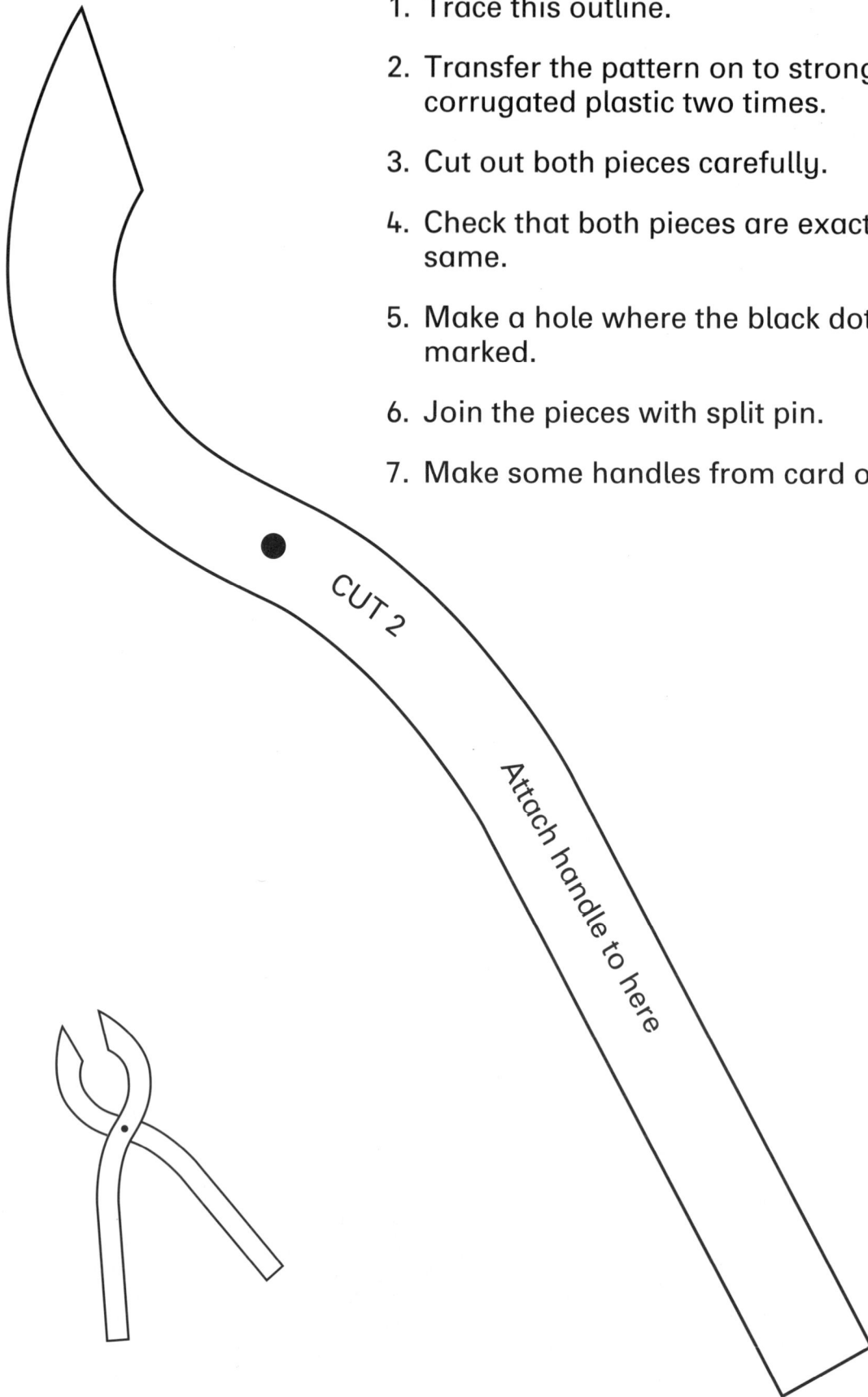

'Helping hand' ▷

1. Trace this outline.

2. Transfer the pattern on to strong card or corrugated plastic two times.

3. Cut out both pieces carefully.

4. Check that both pieces are exactly the same.

5. Make a hole where the black dot is marked.

6. Join the pieces with split pin.

7. Make some handles from card or ramin.

CUT 2

Attach handle to here

A 'tap turner' for Mrs Jacobs ▷

Mrs Jacobs has arthritis in her hands. One task she finds very difficult is turning on a tap. Can you design and make a device to help her?

Answer these questions. The answers should give you some good ideas for your design.

1. What shape are tap heads?

2. How will the device grip the taps?

3. What materials could you use to make it?

4. Should you be able to use the device with one hand?

Great inventions ▷

Cut out the squares carefully. Match each invention to the correct piece of information.

5000 BC *The wheel* This invention made it much easier to move things. It was used for making pottery too.		**1885 AD** *Cars.* Two Germans working in separate places built the first cars. These inventors were called Daimler and Benz.	
3500 BC *Sails* This was the first time that the wind was used to move things along.		**1903 AD** *Aeroplanes* Orville Wright, from America, made the first flight in a plane. The flight lasted for 12 seconds.	
1802 AD *Steam ships* The first one was built in Scotland but was never used!		**1939 AD** *Jet aeroplanes* The first jet plane flew was built in Germany by Hans von Ohain.	
1825 AD *Steam trains* The first railway line was 64 km long. It ran from Stockton to Darlington.		**1961 AD** *Space travel* A Russian astronaut called Yuri Gagarin was the first person in space.	
1873 AD *Bicycles* Mr Lawson invented the first bicycle with a chain. Soon, everyone wanted one.		**1976 AD** *Supersonic aeroplanes* The first passenger aeroplane tofly faster than the speed of sound was Concorde.	

Wheels, axle bearings and hubcaps

Axle bearings

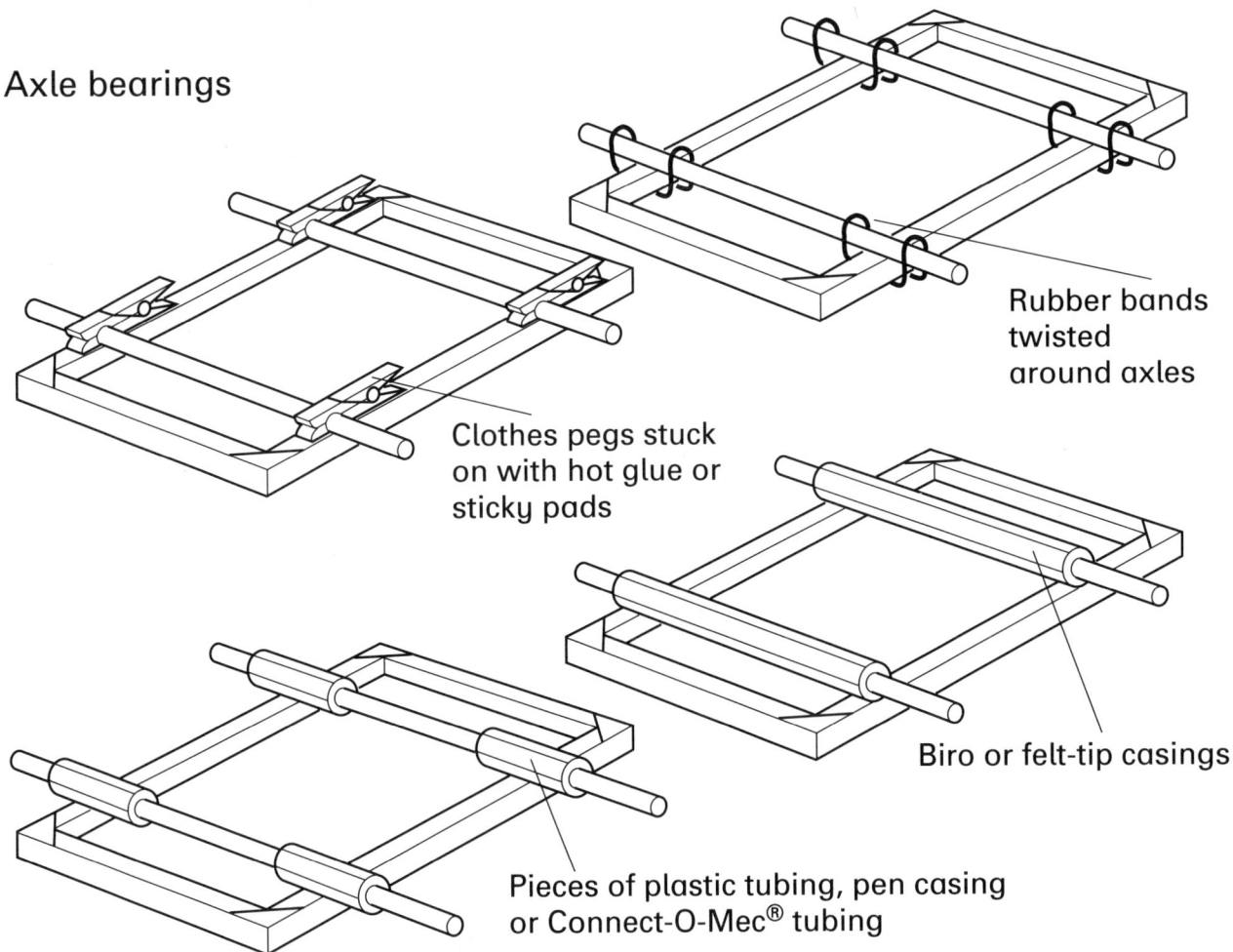

Rubber bands twisted around axles

Clothes pegs stuck on with hot glue or sticky pads

Biro or felt-tip casings

Pieces of plastic tubing, pen casing or Connect-O-Mec® tubing

Wheels

Corrugated cardboard

Jam jar lid

Ping-pong ball

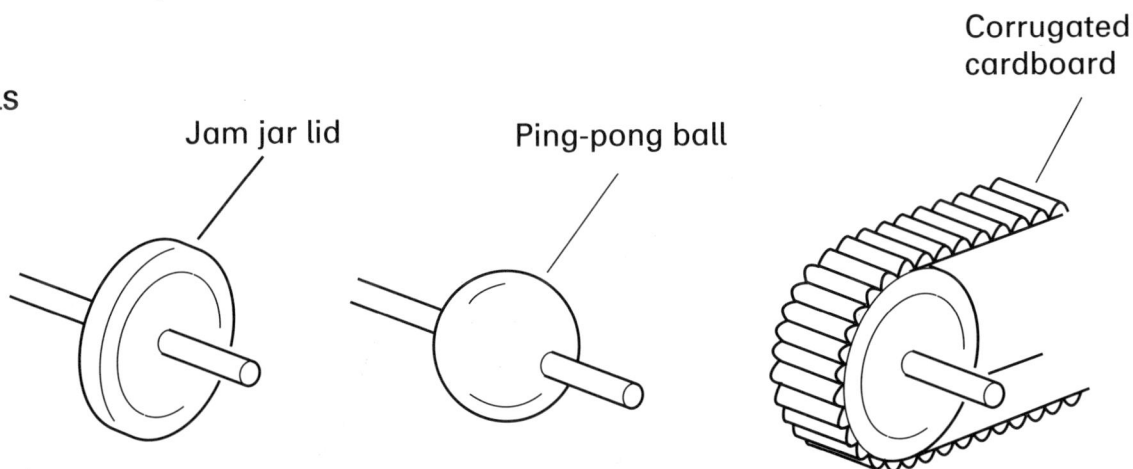

Hubcaps

Plastic tubing

Rubber band or tape

Bead

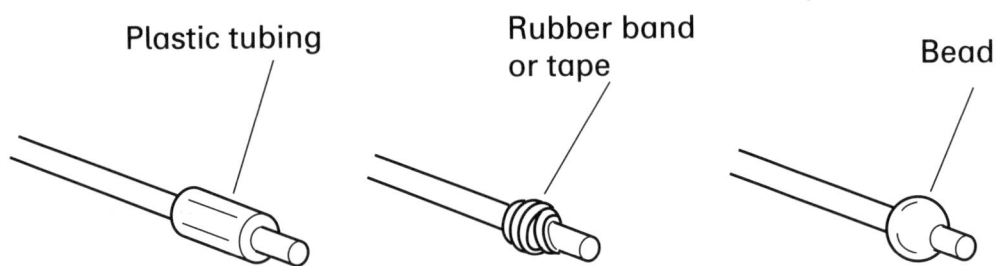

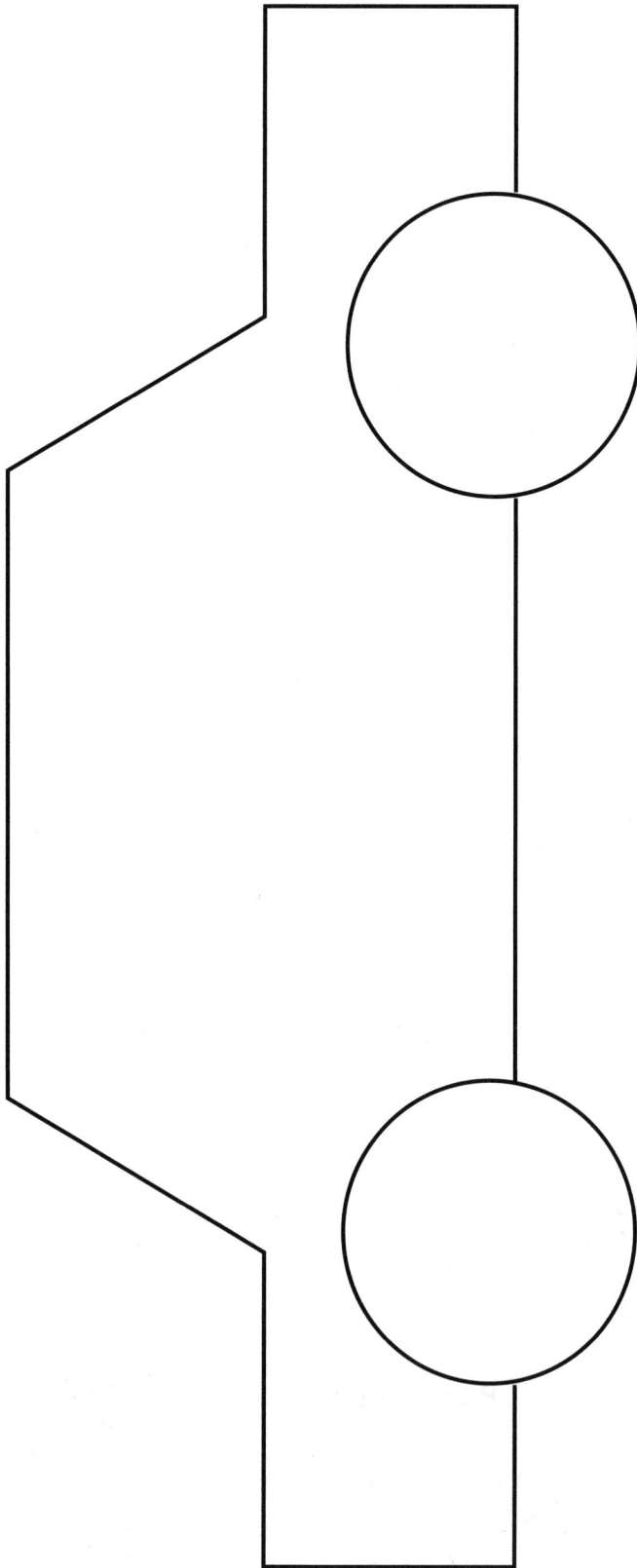

Name _____

Design for my car

Character: _____

Name: _____

Name _____

Making my car

Number these sentences to show the correct order.

Stick the first side together using card corners.

Position the pieces in a rectangle shape.

Cut two shorter lengths of wood using a junior hacksaw.

Mark the wood with a pencil.

Cut some card triangles for the corners.

Use a ruler to measure the wood.

Turn the frame over and stick corners on the second side.

Are there any parts missing?

Write or draw a *better* recipe to show how you are going to make your car. Use the sentences above and these pictures to help you.

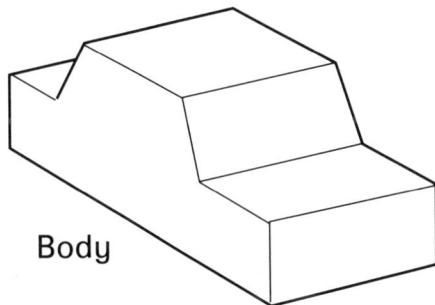

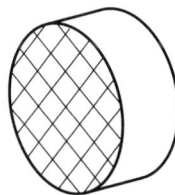

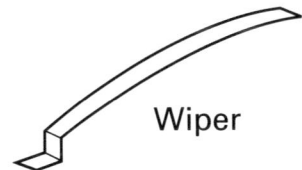

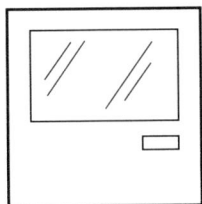

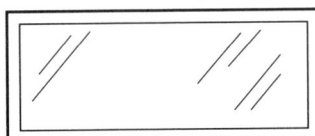

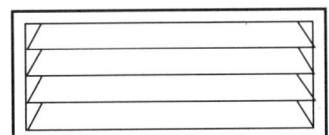

Body

Headlamp

Wiper

Door

NOD 1

Number plate

Mudguard

Bumper

Windscreen

Radiator

Net for a car body

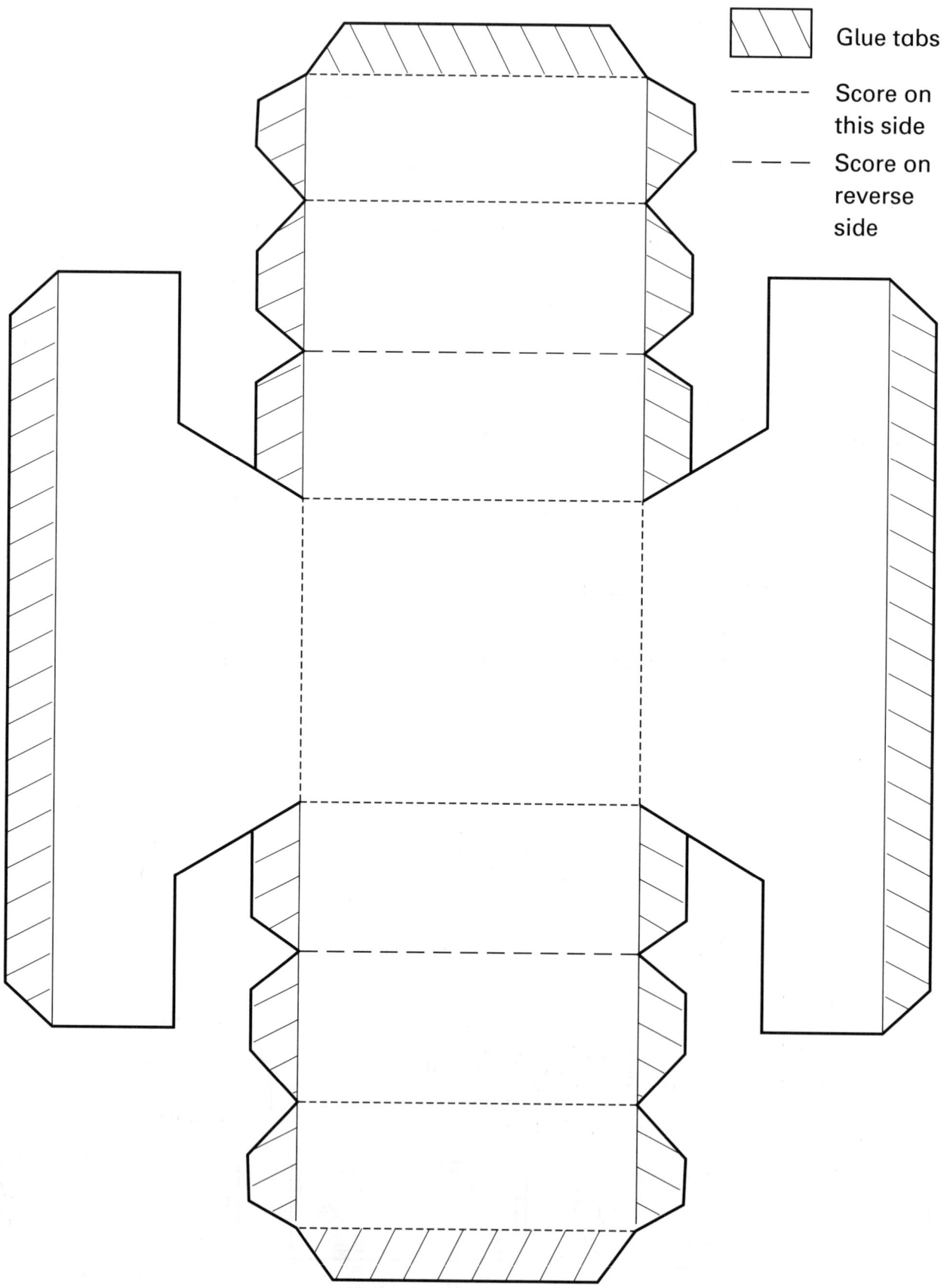

Glue tabs

- - - - - Score on this side

– – – Score on reverse side

Name _____

Evaluation of my car

My design was neatly drawn.

My step-by-step plan was correct.

I remembered to collect all of the equipment on my resources list.

I listened to instructions.

The chassis was straight.

My cardboard net was cut out neatly.

My gluing was careful and neat.

My colouring and decorations were neatly done.

My finished car matched my design.

My car moves well.

I worked on my own with little help.

Name _____

Which material?

Match the materials to what they can be used to make. Some materials can be used for more than one thing. The first one has been done for you.

Table

Cup

Raincoat

Blanket

Take-away container

Bus shelter

Post box

Name badge

Clipboard

Desk-tidy

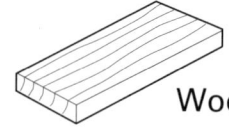 Wood

 Feather

 Plastic

 Glass

 Fabric

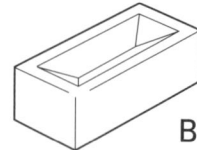 Paper

 Brick

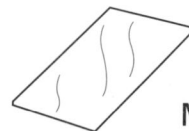 Clay

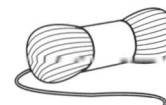 Metal

Wool

Copymaster 80

Name _____

Properties of materials

These words can be used to describe the materials in the table below. Write them in the correct columns. You could use some words more than once. The first one has been done for you.

warm   cold   shiny

hard   durable   curved

dull   straight   rigid   flexible

soft   rough   smooth   waterproof

light

translucent   opaque   heavy   fragile

absorbent   strong   able to be cut   transparent

Wood	Kitchen paper	Metal

Cling film

flexible

Name _____

Testing materials ▷

1. Cut similarly sized pieces of correx, kitchen roll and lined paper. Use a pipette to drop three drops of water on to each. Measure and compare the puddles made. Write your results in this table.

Material	Puddle made
correx	
kitchen paper	
lined paper	

2. Cut similar lengths of correx, wood and lined paper. Support the pieces on two piles of books with the ends weighted. Test the strips to see how much weight they will hold. Write your results in this table.

Material	Weight held
correx (channels running along strip)	
wood	
lined paper	
correx (channels running across strip)	

Name _____

The strength of materials ▷

Cut similarly sized pieces of correx, wool fabric, cardboard and kitchen paper.

Fix them to a base using drawing pins or staples.

Wrap a strip of sandpaper around a sanding block and rub each piece of material.

Write your observations in this table.

Material	after 10 rubs	after 50 rubs	after 100 rubs
correx			
fabric			
cardboard			
kitchen paper			

Pulley wheels

Draw an arrow ⌒➤ or ➤⌒ to show which way each wheel turns. Start at 1 and end at 15.

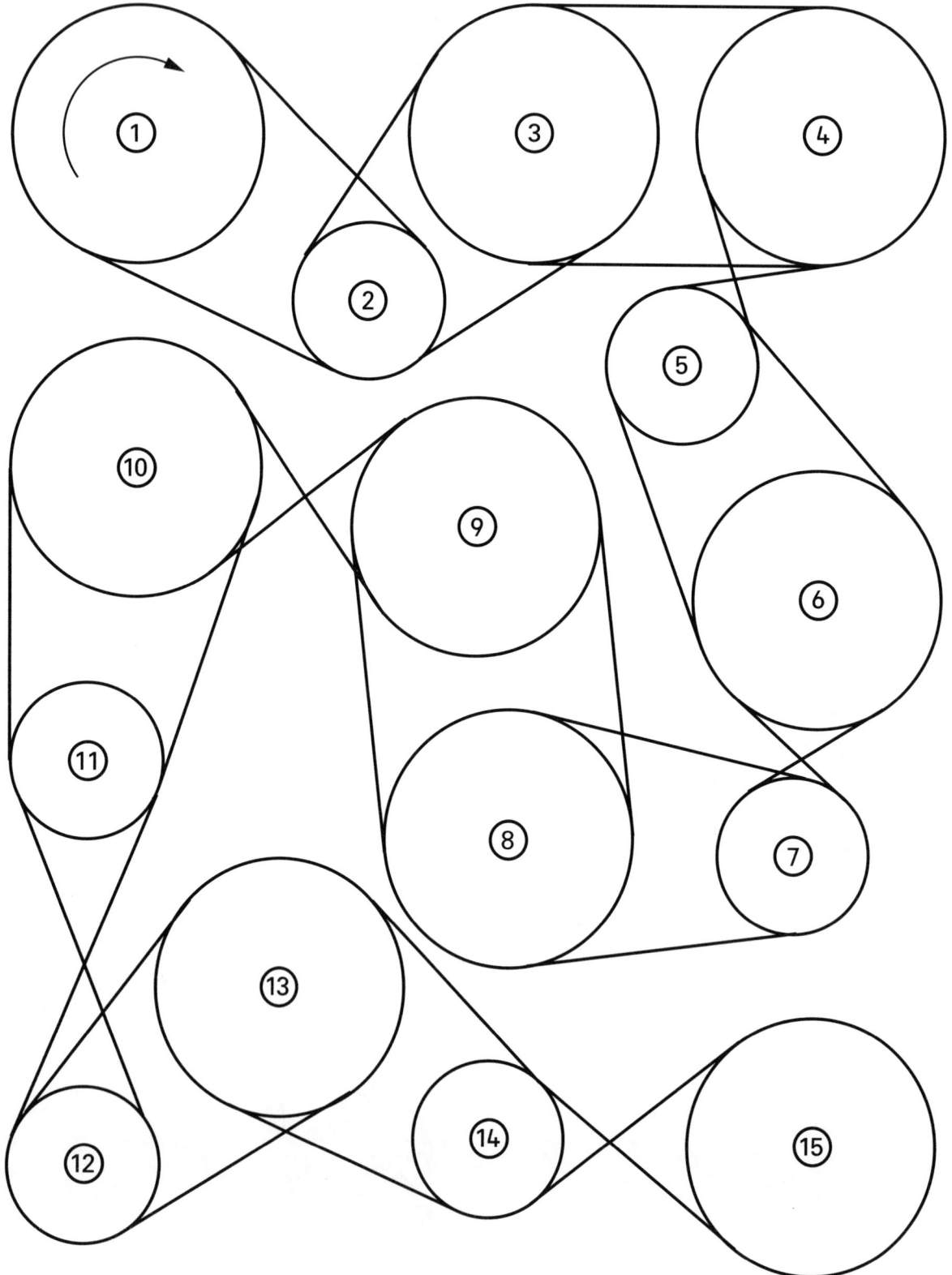

Name _____

Push two pipe cleaners through a straw and bend the ends.

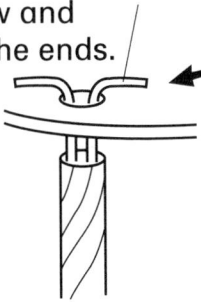

Pipe cleaners or wires keep seats still, or strings allow seats to swing out.

Glue around edges – not to post

To keep cotton reels straight, put them on post before sticking

Card wheels

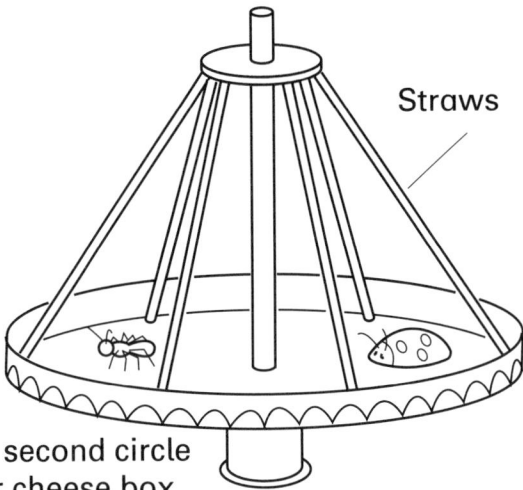

Straws

A circle of correx or a paper plate can be glued directly on to cotton reel

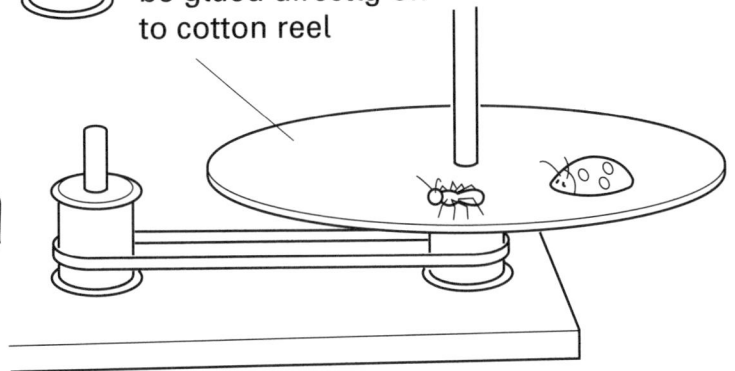

A second circle or cheese box can be used to make drum shape

Bead on top

A cone of card can be stuck to a canopy

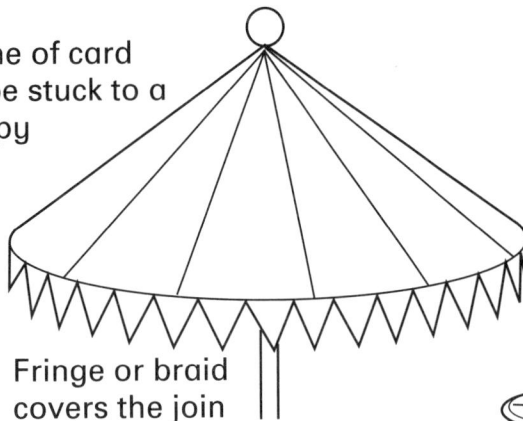

Fringe or braid covers the join

Remember that the decorations must not stick to the dowel post.

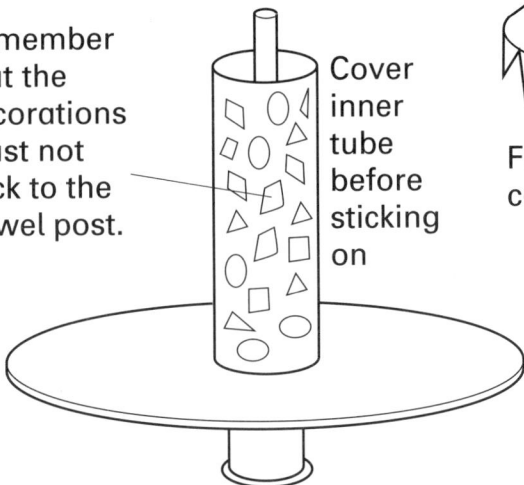

Cover inner tube before sticking on

Use a small piece of dowel or Connect-O-Mec® tubing for handle

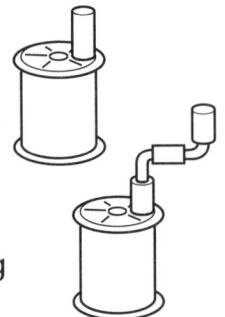

Copymaster 85

Name _____

Roundabout design

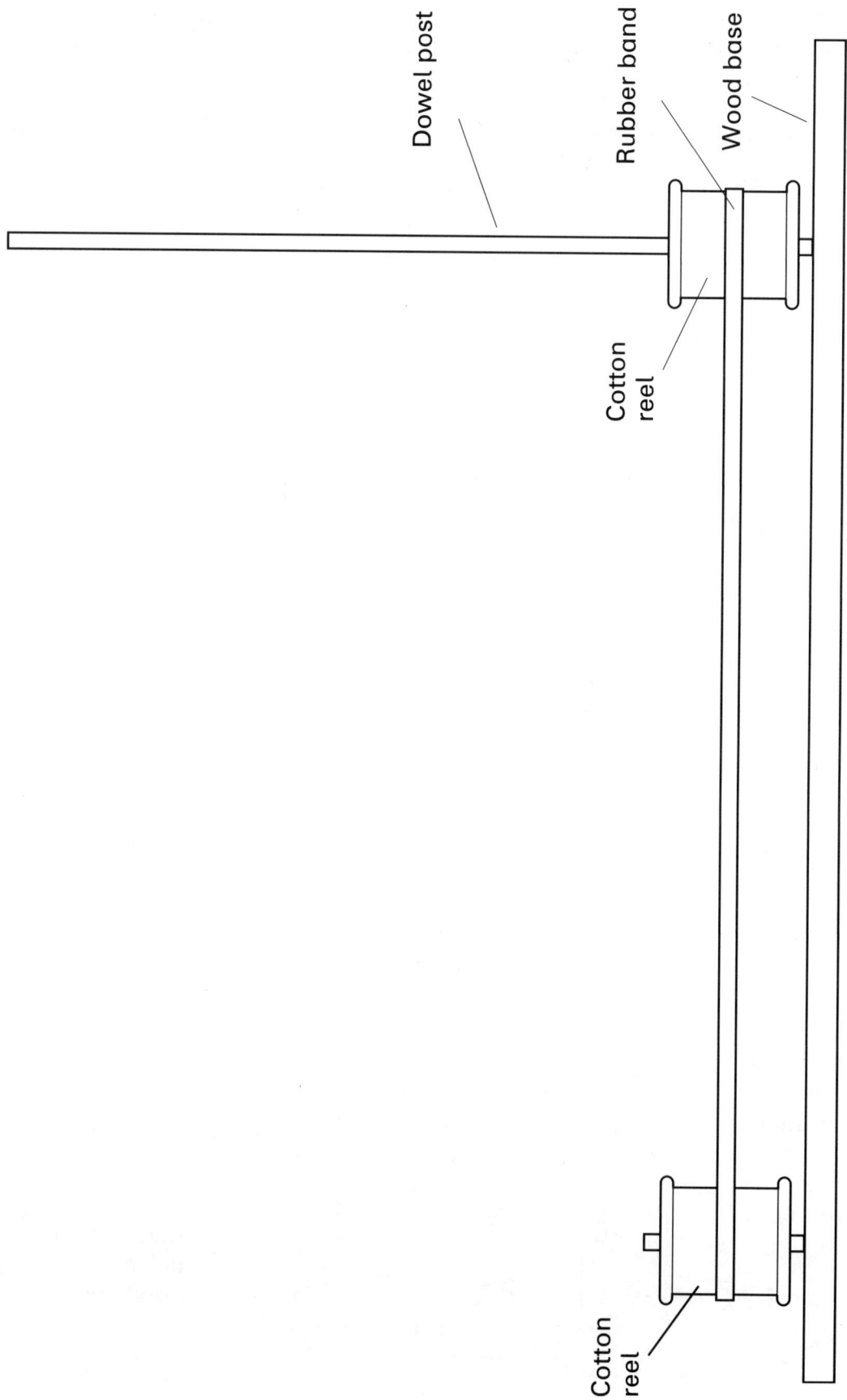

Dowel post

Rubber band

Wood base

Cotton reel

Cotton reel

Gearing up

On each diagram, label whether the wheels at B are turning faster, slower or at the same speed as those at A.

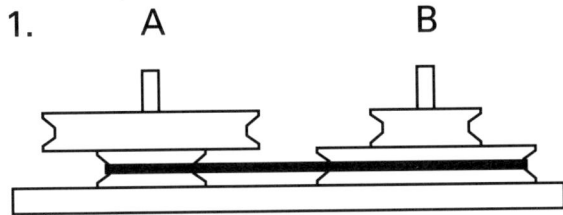

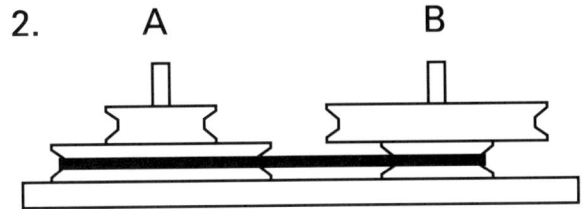

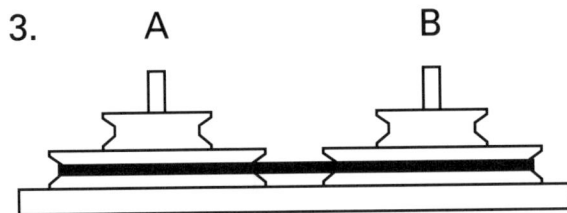

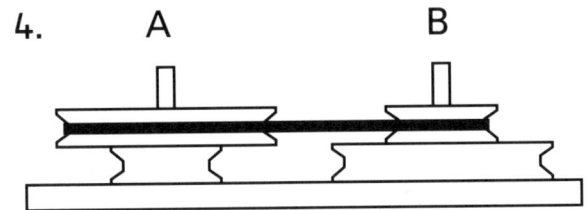

1.   A   B

2.   A   B

3.   A   B

4.   A   B

On each of these diagrams, label whether the wheels at C are turning faster, slower or at the same speed as those at A.

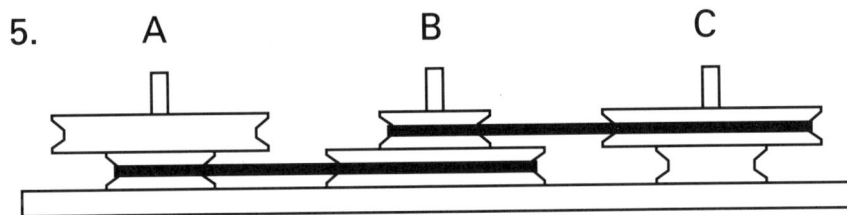

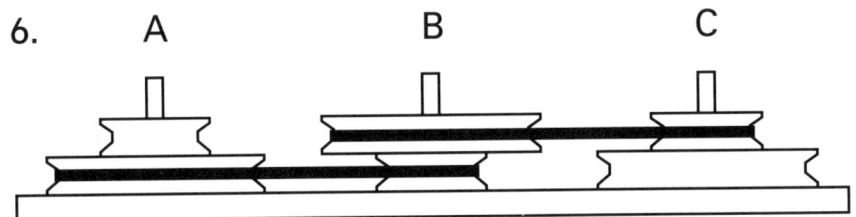

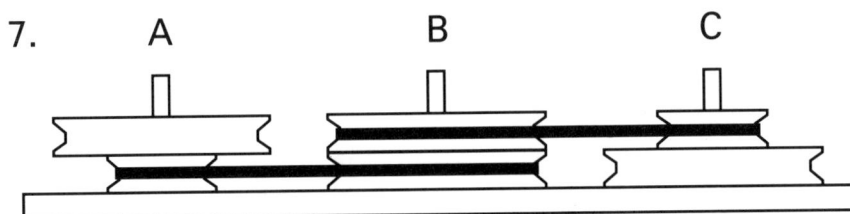

5.   A   B   C

6.   A   B   C

7.   A   B   C

Copymaster 87

Lettering styles

ABCDEFGHIJKLMN
OPQRSTUVWXYZ
abcdefghijklmnopqr
stuvwxyz

ABCDEFGHHIJK

ABCDEFGHIJKLMNOP
QRSTUVWXYZ

ABCDEFGHIJKLMN
OPQRSTUVWXYZ

ABCDEFGHIJKLM
NOPQRSTUVWXYZ

ABCDEFGHIJKLMNOPQ
RSTUVWXYZ

ABCDEFGHIJKLMNOPQRSTUVWXYZ
abcdefghijklmnopqrstuvwxyz

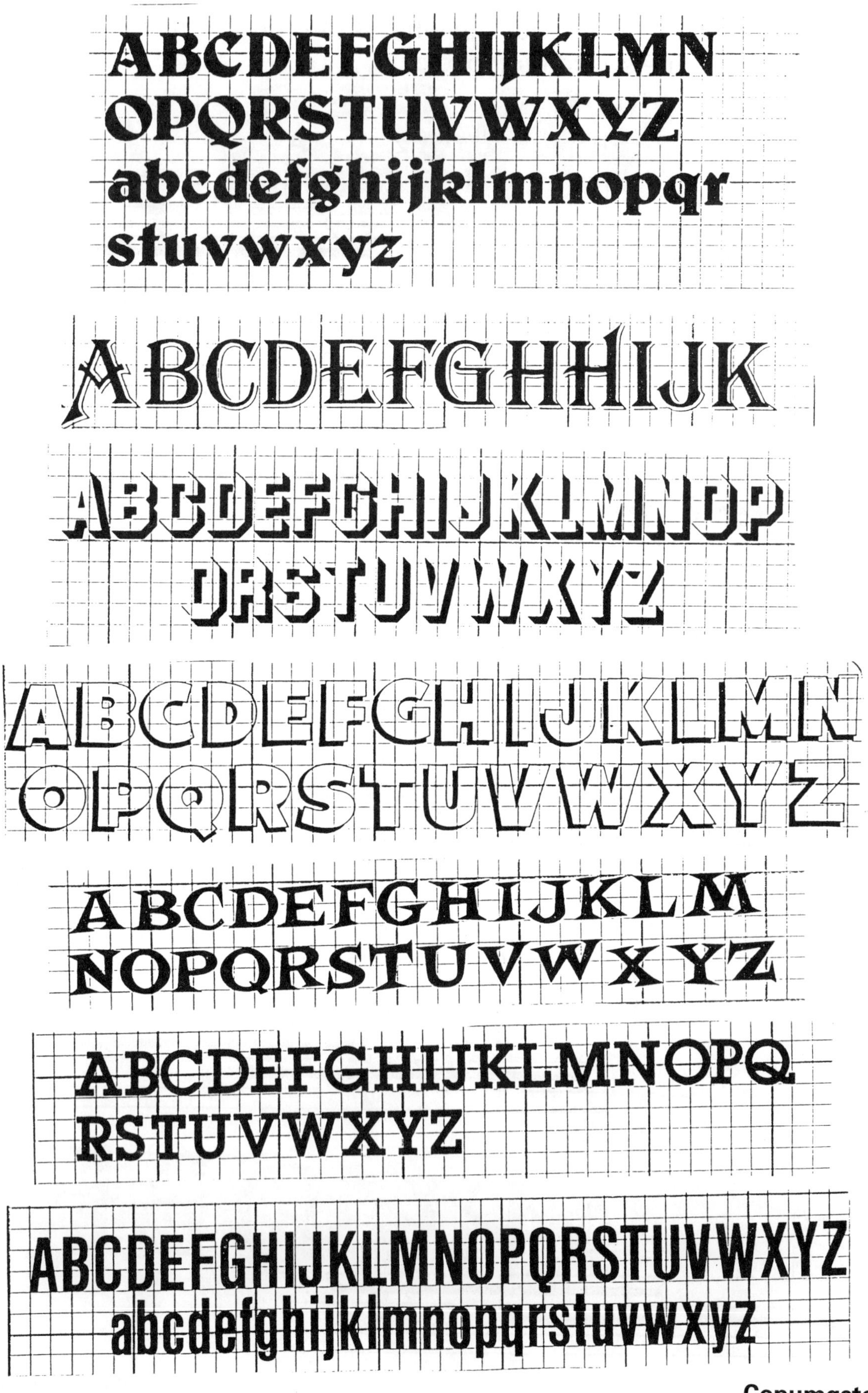

More lettering styles

ABCDEF

ABCDEF

ABCDEF

ABCDEF

ABCDEF

ABCDEF

ABCDEF

ABCDEF

ABCDEF

ABCDEF

ABCDEF

ABCDEF

ABCDEF

Name _____

 wine

 Pizza

BUTCHER

 woolshop

 ToYS

 FiSH shop

 ICes

sport

 HOLIDAYS

How to make a 'cam clown' 1

1. Drill a 4.5 mm hole in a 50mm MDF wheel – but not in the centre.

cam wheel   4.5 mm hole

2. Measure the width of your box, and cut a piece of 4.5 mm dowel 3 cm longer, to make an axle.

3. Measure and mark two spots in the centre of two sides of your box. Make sure they are opposite each other.

4. Drill holes in the sides of the box with a paper drill, and assemble the axle inside.

5. Make sure the axle goes through the off-centre hole, and then glue the wheel securely to the axle.

6. Drill another off-centre hole in a smaller, 30 mm, MDF wheel. Cut a 2 cm piece of dowel and stick it into the off-centre hole.

7. Stick the smaller wheel to one end of axle to make a handle. Stick a piece of plastic tubing or a bead to other end of the axle to act as a stop.

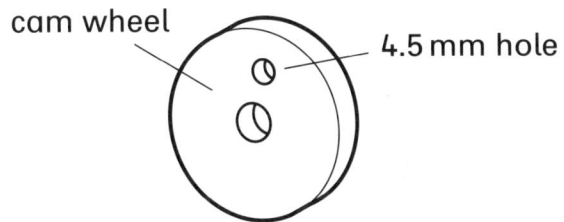

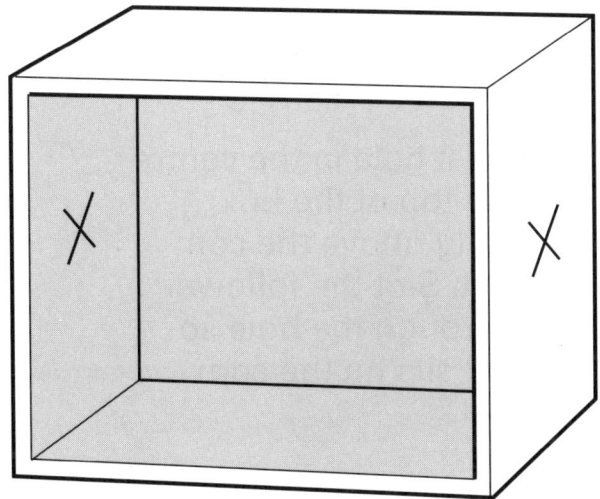

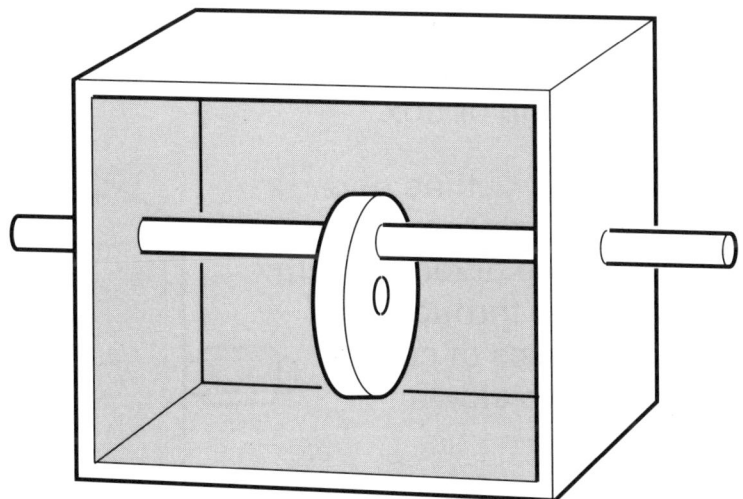

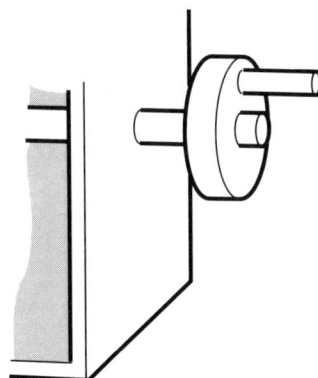

How to make a 'cam clown' 2

8. Cut a piece of dowel the same length as the space between the top of the box and the axle (x) plus 10 cm.

9. Stick a 50 mm MDF wheel to one end, placing the dowel in the centre hole.

10. Make a hole in the centre of the top of the box, directly above the cam wheel. Slot the follower up through the hole so that it sits on the cam wheel.

11. Check the movement of the follower, and if it wobbles, slot a cotton reel over the dowel and stick to top of box.

12. Draw the outline of a clown's face on thin card. It must be at least 10 cm high. Cut through two thicknesses of card to make two clown faces.

13. Decorate the outlines so they look like the front and back of a clown's head. Sandwich the spindle between the two pieces of card with glue.

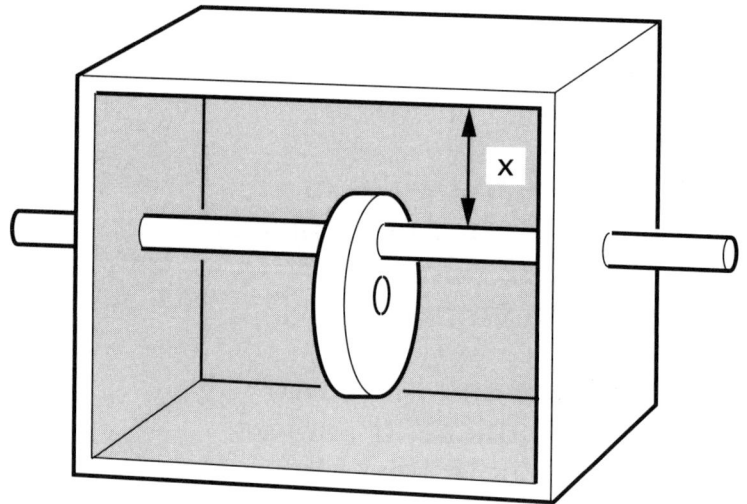

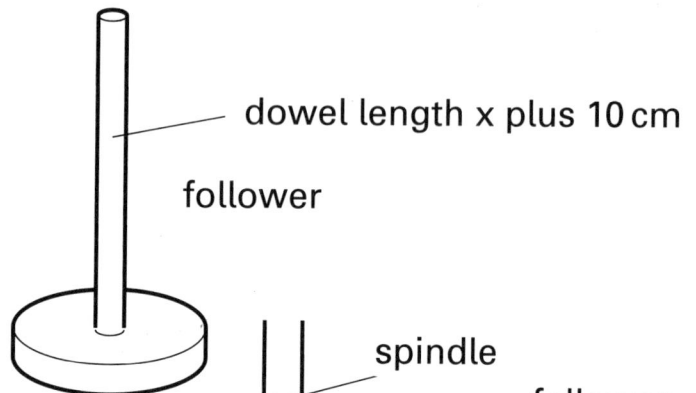

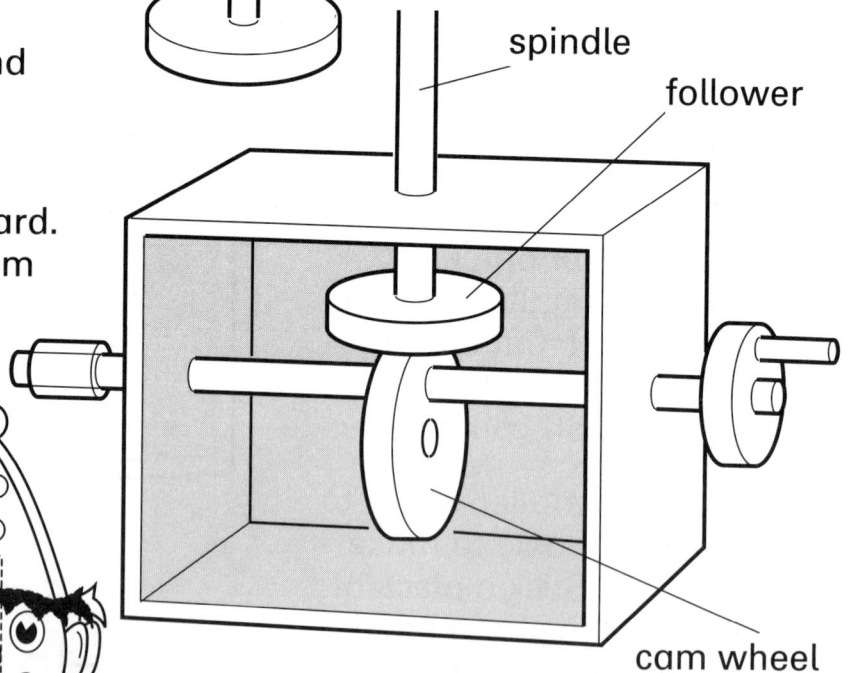

x

dowel length x plus 10 cm

follower

spindle

follower

cam wheel

Name _____

1. Make two holes in the sides of a box with a paper drill. Make sure that the holes are directly opposite each other.

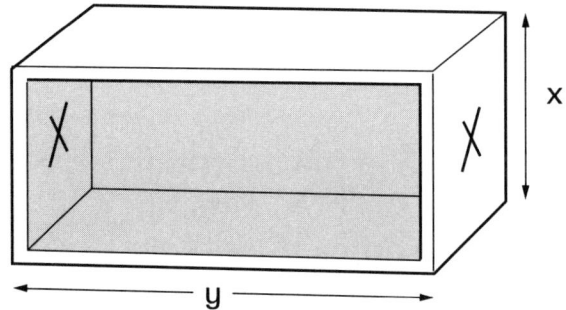

2. Cut a piece of wire 10 cm longer than the box (y plus 10 cm).

3. Mark and bend the middle of the wire, as shown, using pliers.

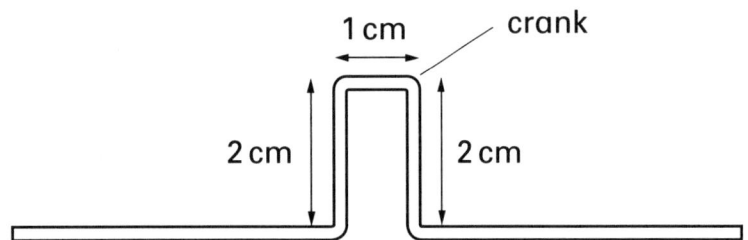

4. Cut a piece of 5 mm plastic tubing 3 cm long, and make a hole through one end with a revolving punch.

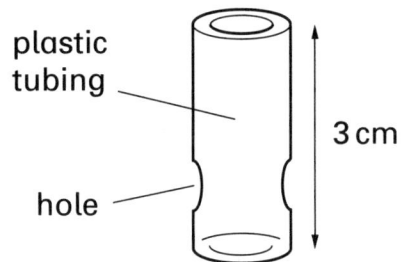

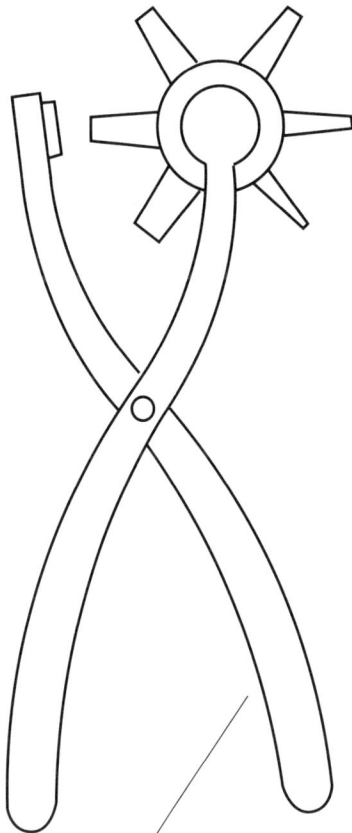

revolving punch

5. Push the wire through one side of the box, then through the hole in the plastic tubing and out through the other side of the box.

6. Trim the ends of the wire, if necessary, and stick a bead on each end.

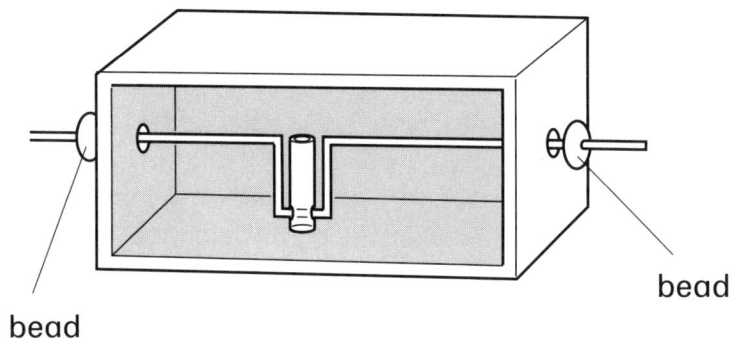

bead

bead

How to make a 'crank creature' 2 ▷

7. Cut a length of 4.5 mm dowel the same height as the box (x).

8. Drill a hole in the centre of the top of the box, directly above the crank. Slot the dowel through the hole and push it into the plastic tubing. Secure the dowel with glue if it is loose.

9. Test the mechanism, and if the shaft does not move, cut a longer slot from the front to the back of the box top.

10. Draw an animal shape on thin card. Cut through two thicknesses of card to make two animal shapes.

11. Decorate the shapes so that they look like the front and back of the animal. Stick these to the dowel follower so that the shaft is sandwiched between the two pieces of card.

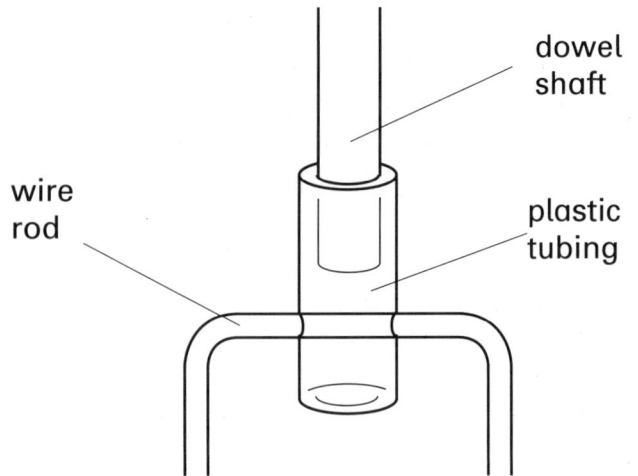

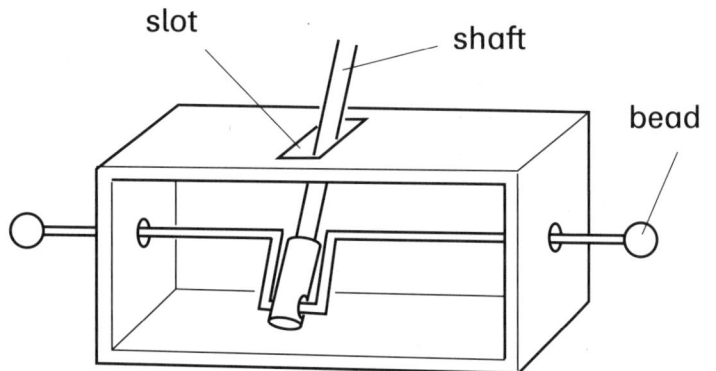

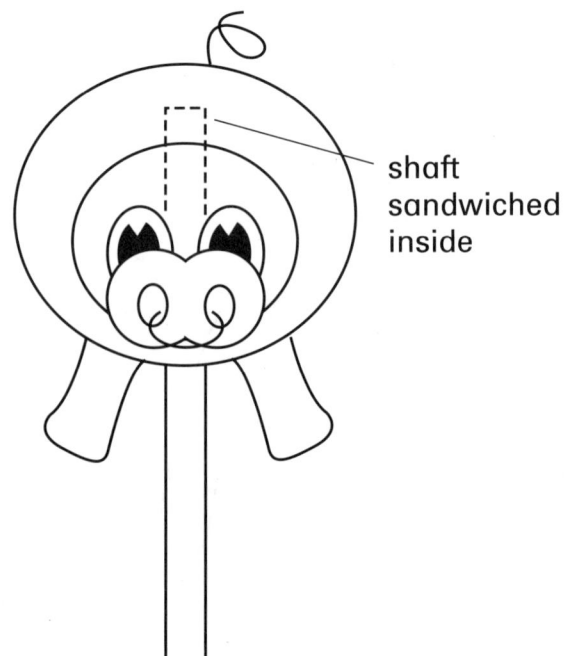

dowel shaft

wire rod

plastic tubing

slot

shaft

bead

shaft sandwiched inside

Assembly instructions for minibeast kit ▷

Assembly instructions for minibeast kit

Contents:

1.	2.
3.	4.
5.	6.

Name _____

Dear _____ ,

During this term's Design & Technology project I will be making

_____

I will need to bring

_____

_____

_____

_____

Please return the form below if you can provide the materials that I will need.

Thank you for helping me,

✂ -

Name of child _____ Date _____

I am able to provide the materials that my child will need.

Signed _____

Name _____

Dear Parents,

As part of our Design & Technology programme, Class_____

will be making _____

We would be grateful if you could make a voluntary contribution

of_____ to cover the cost of the materials used.

Please return the form below with any contribution that you
make.

Yours sincerely,

✂ -

Name of child _____ Date _____

I enclose a voluntary contribution of _____ to cover the
cost of materials.

Signed _____

Letter to parents 3

Dear Parents,

As part of our Food Technology programme, Class _____

will be carrying out food tests on _____ , during

which we will be tasting the following foods:

_____

_____

_____

Please complete the form below, or contact the school, if your child has any special dietary requirements or if you have any other queries regarding this activity.

Yours sincerely,

✂ -

Name of child _____ Date _____

Dietary requirements: _____

Signed _____

Name _____

Dear _____

I will be doing Food Technology on _____

and I will be making _____

Please will you make a voluntary contribution of _____
towards the cost of the ingredients.

Please contact the school if I have any special dietary
requirements or if you have any other questions about this
activity.

Thank you for helping me,

✂ -

Name of child _____ Date _____

I enclose a voluntary contribution of _____ to cover the
cost of ingredients.

Signed _____

Name _____

Dear _____

I will be doing Food Technology on _____

and I will be making _____

I will need to bring _____

_____

_____

_____

I will be eating my food at school.

Please return the form below if you can provide the ingredients that I need.

Thank you for helping me,

✂ -

Name of child _____ Date _____

I am able to provide the ingredients that my child will need.

Signed _____

Design & Technology poster

Can you help?

During our Design & Technology work this term we need the following items:

_____
_____
_____
_____
_____
_____

If you can help us, please would you speak to :

_____
_____
_____

Name _____

Project ideas

Initial design ideas		
Project		

Name _____

Final design

Final design

Project

Name _____

Planning sheet ▷

Task:

Tools:	Materials:

Other equipment:

Step 1:	Step 2:

Step 3:	Step 4:

Step 5:	Step 6:

Name _____

Resources planning sheet

Task:

Tools I will need:	Materials I will need:

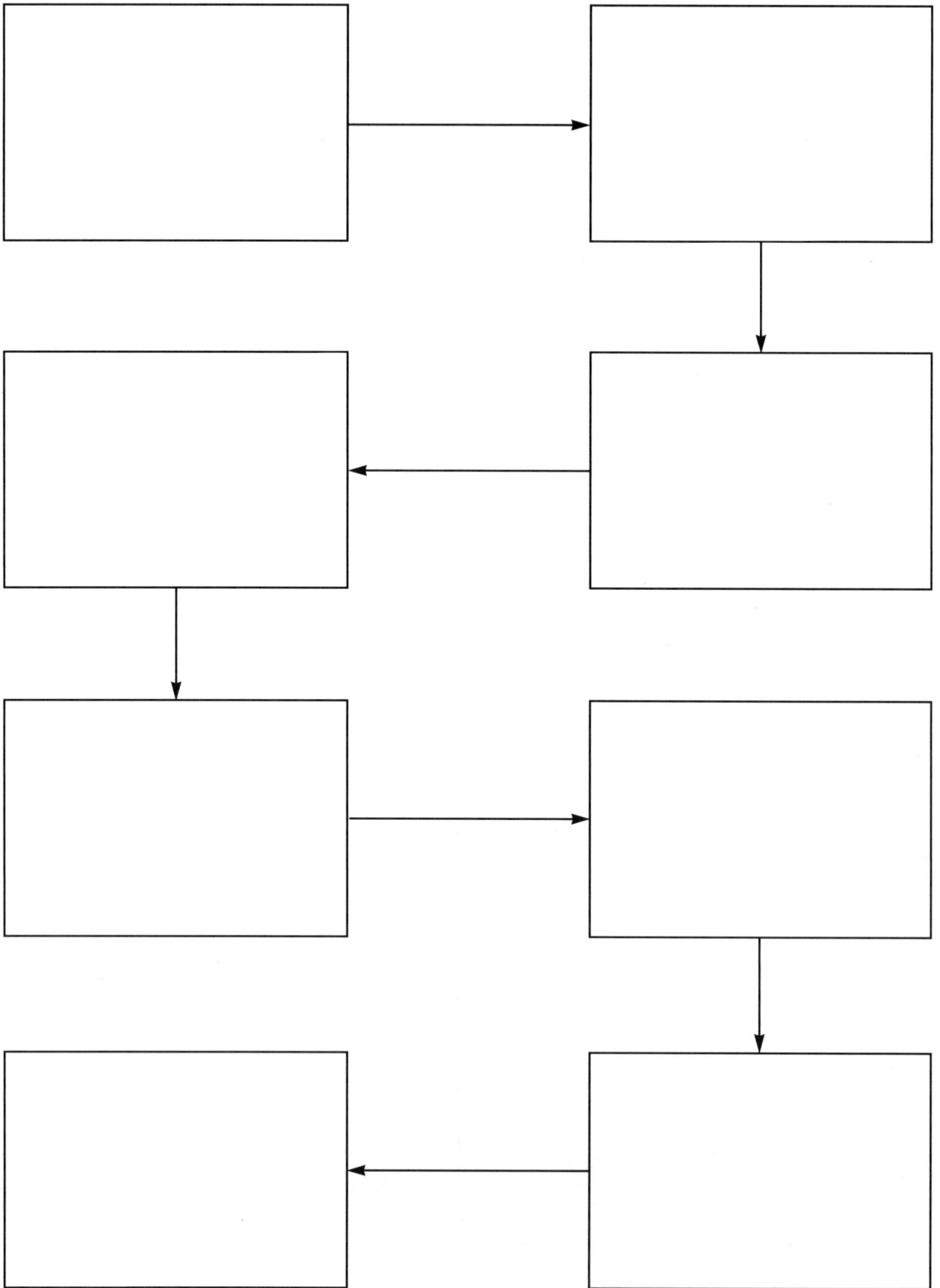

Name _____

Name _____

Evaluating sheet ▷

Task:

Things I found easy:	Things that were hard to do:
New things I learned:	Improvements I could make:

Name _____

Joining

Here are some ways of joining things together.

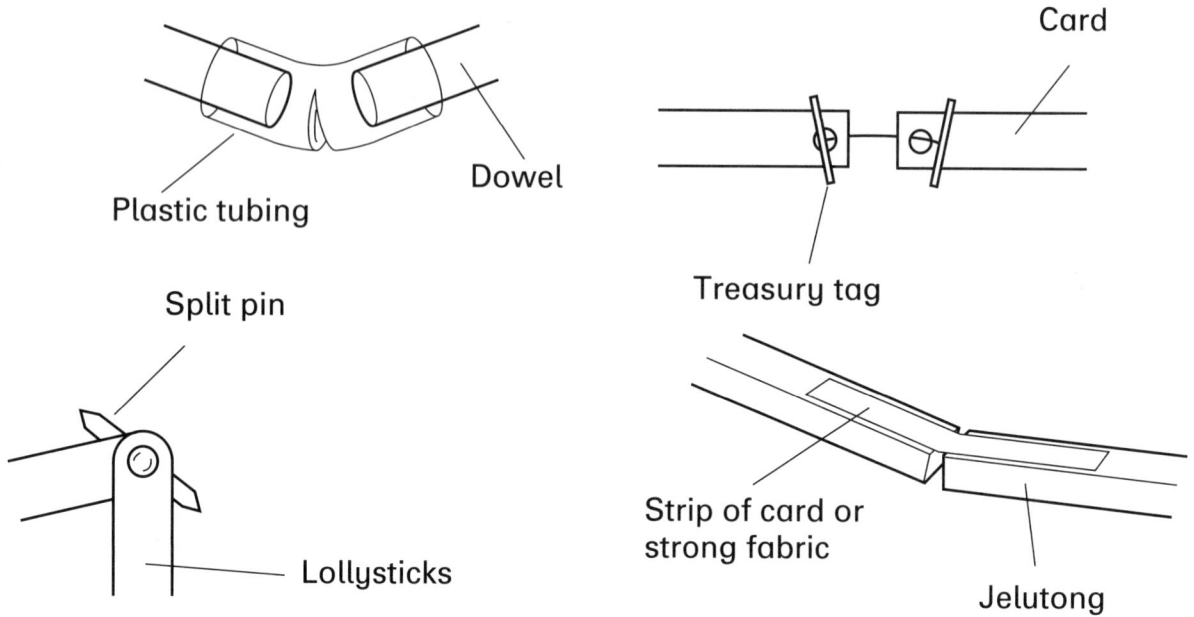

Which of the following methods would you use to join:

a) two pieces of fabric together?

b) two pieces of card together?

c) two pieces of paper together?

d) two pieces of electrical wire together?

e) a picture to a display board?

f) a card triangle to a wooden frame?

g) a poster to the wall?

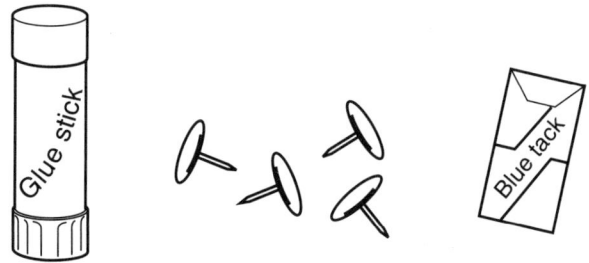

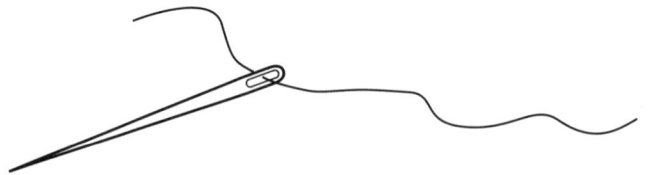

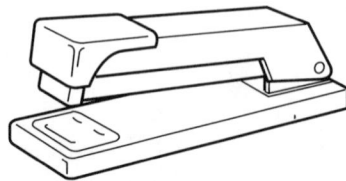

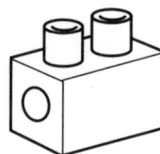

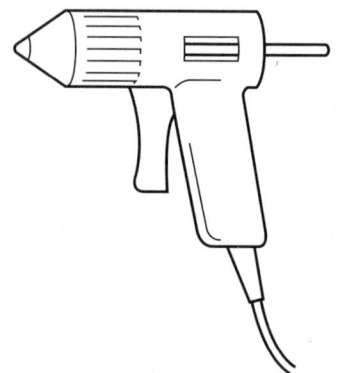

Together forever

Colour red the joining methods which are *permanent* – joined forever.
Colour blue those which are *temporary* – can easily be taken apart and
put back together again without spoiling the materials involved.

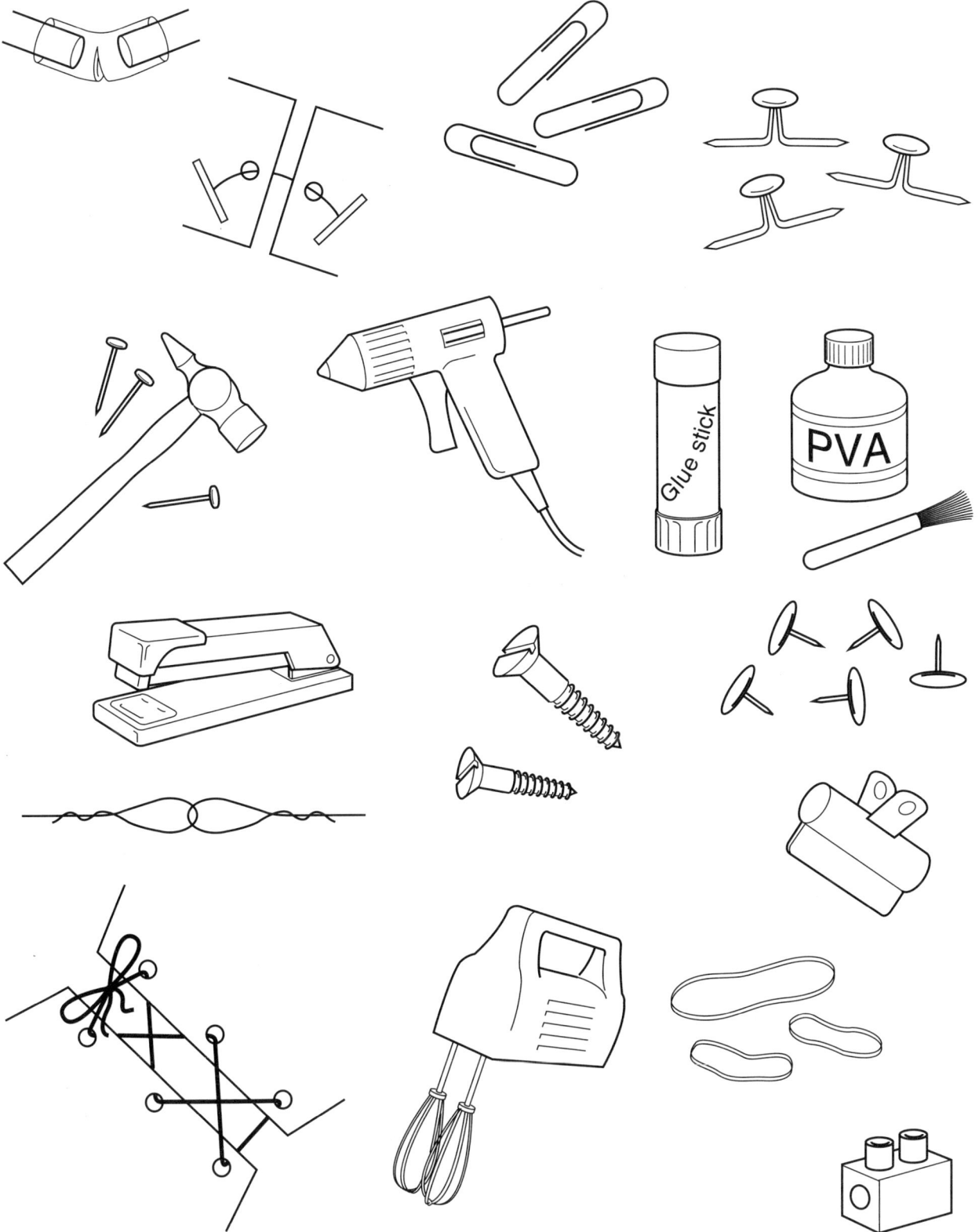

Glue stick

PVA

Cutting

Draw a line from each tool to the material on which you would use it.

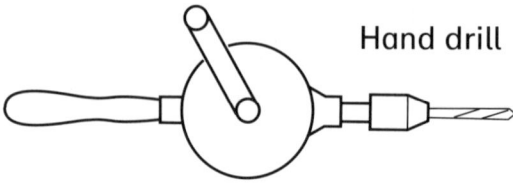

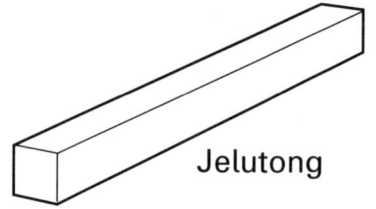

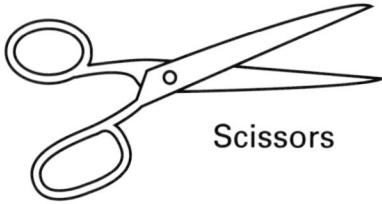

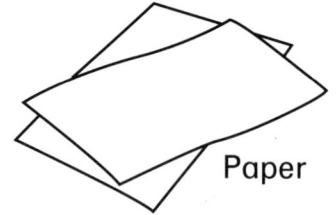

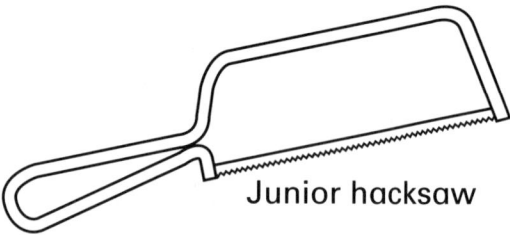

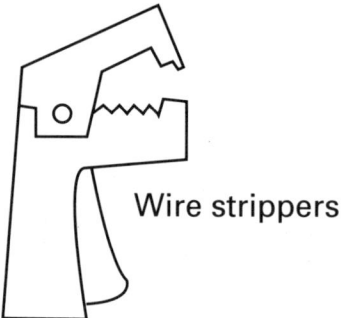

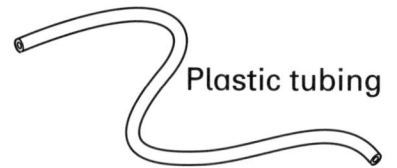

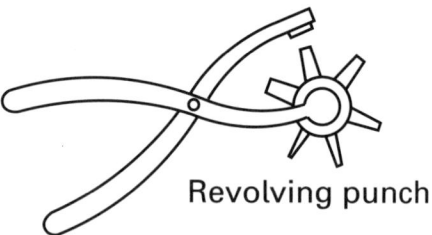

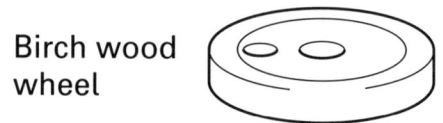

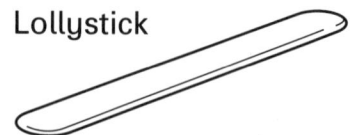

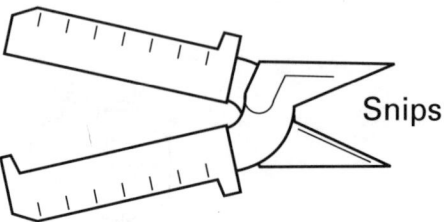

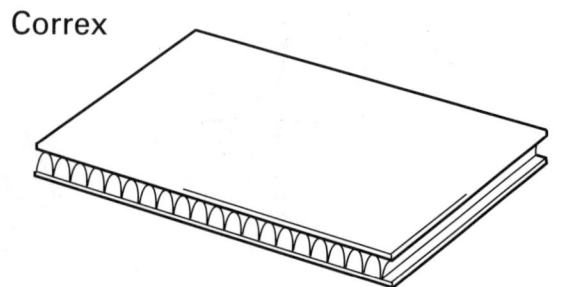

Hand drill

Jelutong

Scissors

Paper

Junior hacksaw

Wire

Wire strippers

Plastic tubing

Birch wood wheel

Revolving punch

Lollystick

Stitch unpicker

Correx

Snips

Name _____

Write the names of these tools in the spaces.

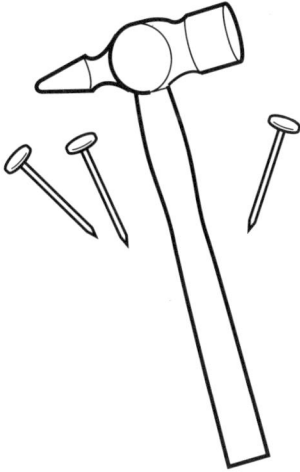

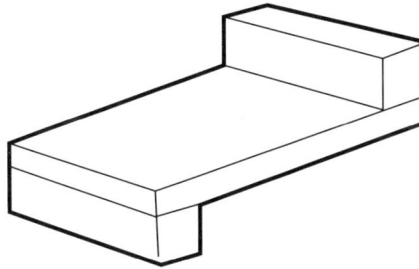

2. _____

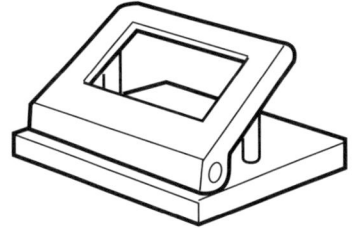

3. _____

1. _____

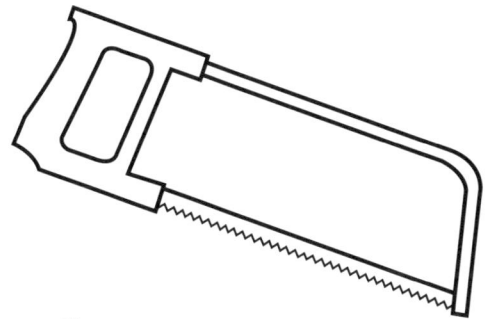

5. _____

4. _____

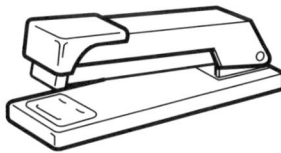

8. _____

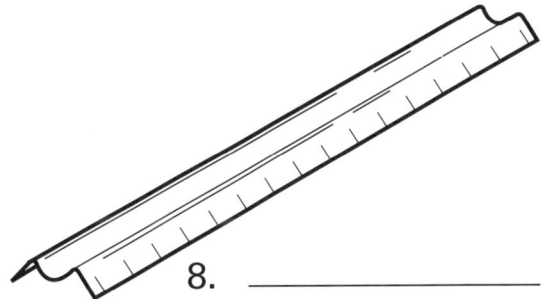

7. _____

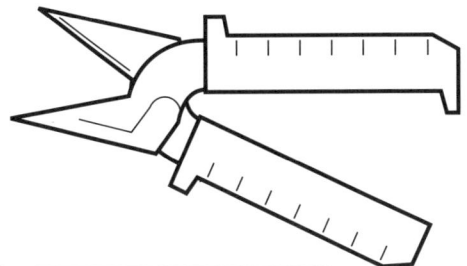

9. _____

6. _____

On a separate piece of paper, write a sentence about each tool to explain what it is used for.

Name _____

Match the names to the correct tools.

1.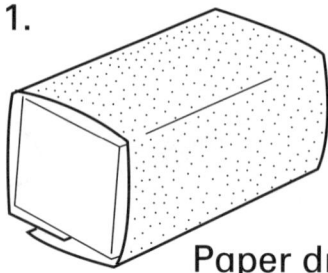
Paper drill

2.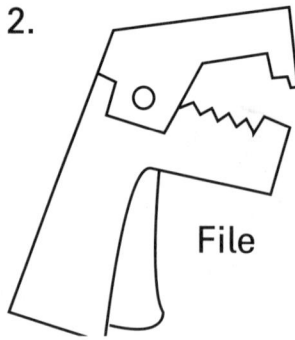
File

3.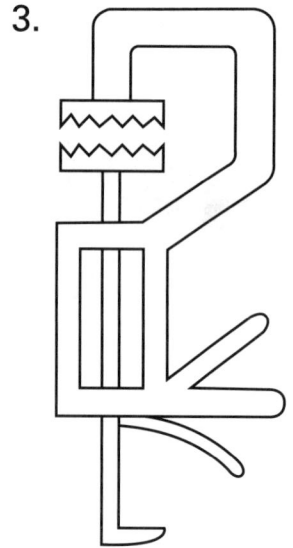
Perforator

4.
Glue gun

5.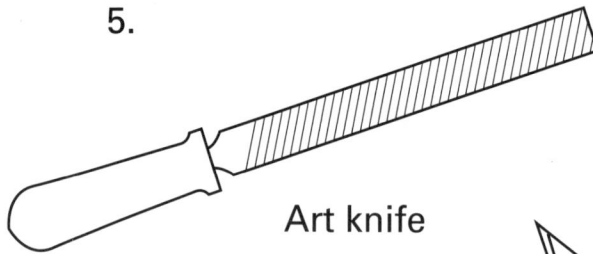
Art knife

6.
Solo clamp

7.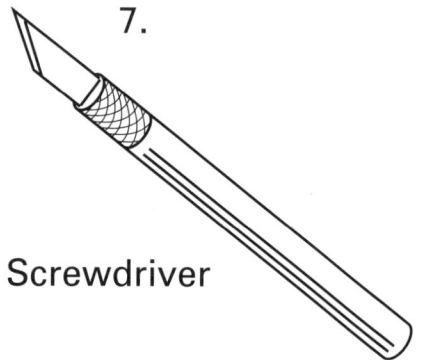
Screwdriver

Sanding block

8.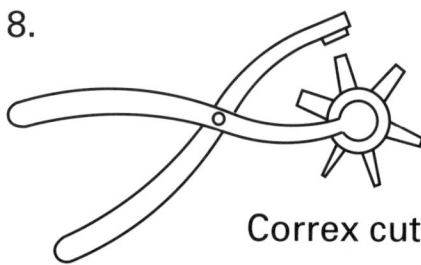
Correx cutter

Rotary punch

9.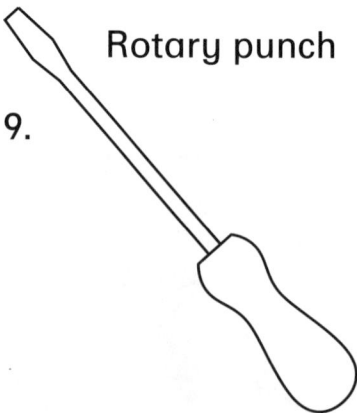

10.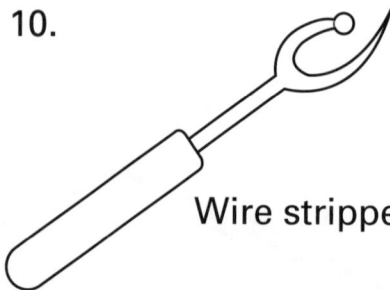
Wire strippers

11.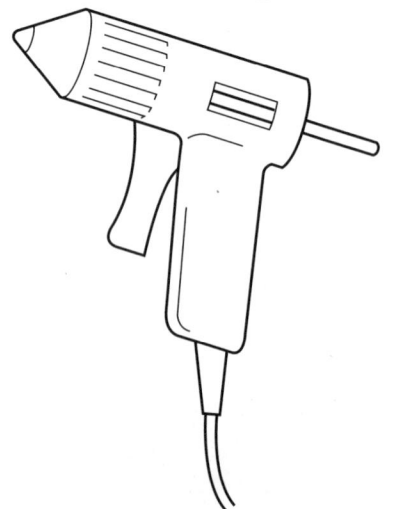

On a separate piece of paper, write a sentence about each tool to explain what it is used for.

Tool silhouettes

Write the name of each tool next to its silhouette.

1.

2.

3.

4.

5.

6.

7.

8.

9.

10.

11.

12.

13.

14.

Name _____

Find the words listed below in the wordsearch. They can be horizontal, vertical, diagonal or backwards. This first one has been done for you.

e.g.

```
        D
(P A P E R)
        I
        L
        L
```

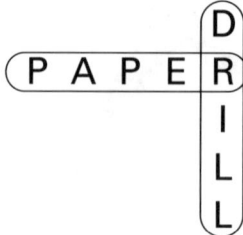

ARTKNIFE
BENCH HOOK
CLAMP
CORREX CUTTER
FILE
GLUE GUN
HACKSAW
HAMMER
HAND DRILL
NEEDLE
PAPER DRILL
PINS
PERFORATOR
PLIERS
REVOLVING PUNCH
RULER
SCREWDRIVER
SCISSORS
SHAPER SAW
SNIPS
SOLDERING IRON
STAPLER
WIRE CUTTER

```
C S N I P H A C K S A W N R D
B O Q J L I R S D U X E U C R
S A S C I S S O R S E L V L R
O G L U E A H A N D E B I A O
L U C W R D E F L R G O P M T
D N H I S L M E O I N V U P A
E X R R W R E V O L V I N G R
R E Q E E A E T U L W C C Y O
I R O N T L S R E M M A H Z F
N R B E I T P R Z S N I P S R
G O N F I J U A E M P F N D E
R C U T T E R C T P A P E R P
B E N C H H O O K S A E A I K
U R E E F I N K T R A H U L N
S C R E W D R I V E R T S L C
```

Name _____

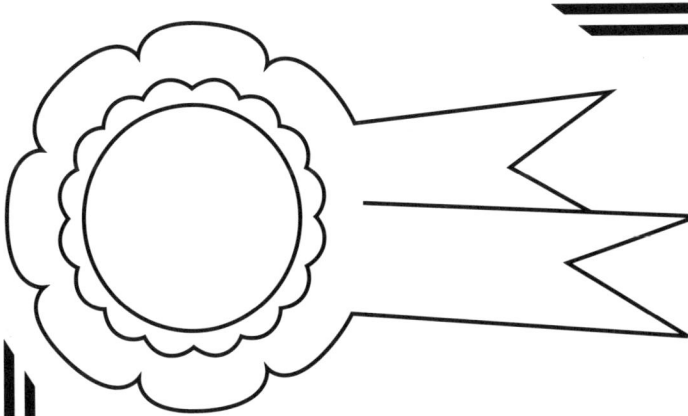

CERTIFICATE FOR DESIGN AND TECHNOLOGY

awarded to

Signed

Date

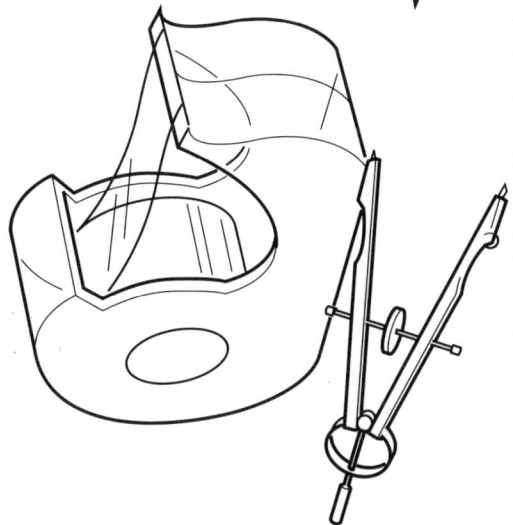

Name _____

Design and Technology Portfolio

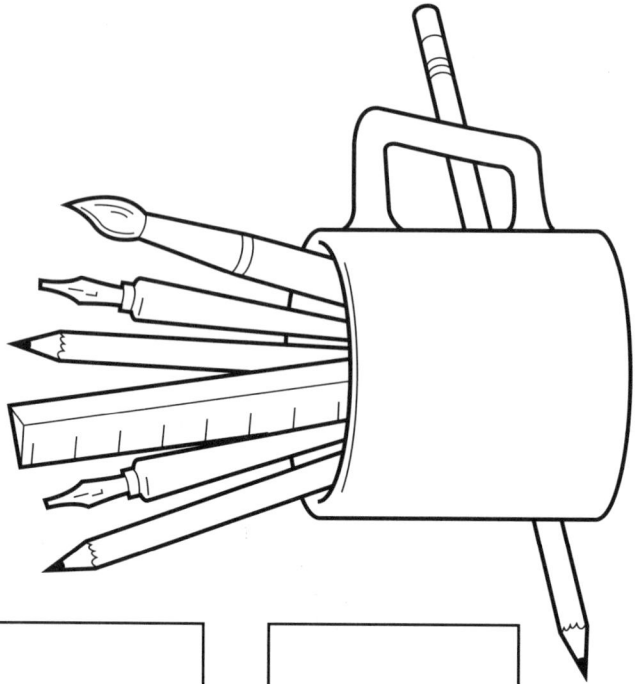

Project:

Name:

Name _____

Isometric paper

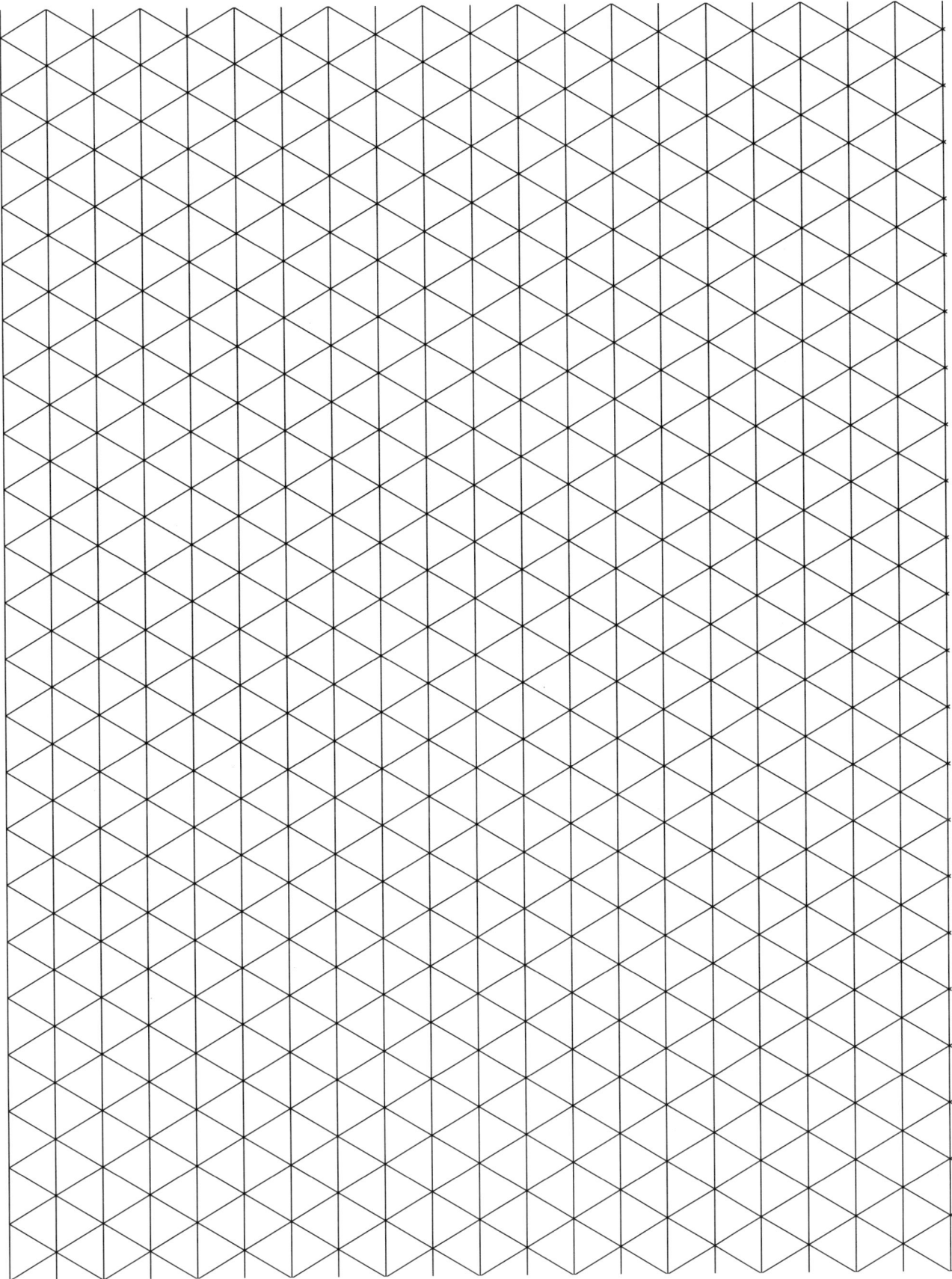

Name _____

Planning checklist ▷

Planning Checklist Year:			
Materials			
Unit 1: Sheet materials			
Unit 2: Frameworks			
Unit 3: Mouldable materials			
Unit 4: Textiles			
Unit 5: Food			
Unit 6: Controlling electricity			
Unit 7: Levers			
Unit 8: Wheels/axles			
Unit 9: Gears/pulleys			
Unit 10: Cams and cranks			
Designing			
use information sources to help their designing generate ideas considering users and purposes			
clarify ideas, develop criteria and suggest ways forward			
consider appearance, function, safety and reliability			
explore, develop and communicate aspects of design by modelling their ideas in a variety of ways			
develop a clear idea of what has to be done, sequence of actions, and alternative ways of proceeding			
evaluate design ideas as these develop, bearing in mind the users and purposes			
Making			
select appropriate materials, tools and techniques			
measure, mark out, cut and shape a range of materials, using additional tools, equipment and techniques			
join and combine materials and components			
apply additional finishing techniques			
planning how to use materials, equipment and processes, and suggesting alternative methods			
evaluate their products, identifying strengths and weaknesses, and carrying out tests			
implement improvements they have identified			
Knowledge and understanding			
how the working characteristics of materials relate to the ways materials are used			
how materials can be combined and mixed to create more useful properties			
how simple mechanisms can be used to produce different movement			
how electrical circuits can be used			
how structures can fail and techniques for reinforcing and strengthening them			
to investigate, disassemble and evaluate simple products and applications			
to relate the way things work to their intended purpose			
to distinguish between how well a product has been made and designed			
to consider the effectiveness of a product			
knowledge and understanding of health and safety			
to use the appropriate vocabulary			

Copymaster 118

Record-keeping sheet

Record-keeping sheet Name:			
Materials Unit 1: Sheet materials			
Unit 2: Frameworks			
Unit 3: Mouldable materials			
Unit 4: Textiles			
Unit 5: Food			
Unit 6: Controlling electricity			
Unit 7: Levers			
Unit 8: Wheels/axles			
Unit 9: Gears/pulleys			
Unit 10: Cams and cranks			
Designing use information sources to help their designing			
generate ideas considering users and purposes			
clarify ideas, develop criteria and suggest ways forward			
consider appearance, function, safety and reliability			
explore, develop and communicate aspects of design by modelling their ideas in a variety of ways			
develop a clear idea of what has to be done, sequence of actions, and alternative ways of proceeding			
evaluate design ideas as these develop, bearing in mind the users and purposes			
Making select appropriate materials, tools and techniques			
measure, mark out, cut and shape a range of materials, using additional tools, equipment and techniques			
join and combine materials and components			
apply additional finishing technique			
planning how to use materials, equipment and processes, and suggesting alternative methods			
evaluate their products, identifying strengths and weaknesses, and carrying out tests			
implement improvements they have identified			
Knowledge and understanding how the working characteristics of materials relate to the ways materials are used			
how materials can be combined and mixed to create more useful properties			
how simple mechanisms can be used to produce different movement			
how electrical circuits can be used			
how structures can fail and techniques for reinforcing and strengthening them			
to investigate, disassemble and evaluate simple products and applications			
to relate the way things work to their intended purpose			
to distinguish between how well a product has been made and designed			
to consider the effectiveness of a product			
knowledge and understanding of health and safety			
to use the appropriate vocabulary			

Copymaster 119